TWISTED TOUR GUIDE
LOS ANGELES
SHOCKING DEATHS, SCANDAL AND VICE

TWISTED TOUR GUIDE TO LOS ANGELES

SHOCKING DEATHS, SCANDALS AND VICE

By Marques Vickers

MARQUIS PUBLISHING
HERRON ISLAND, WASHINGTON

Version 1.1

Published by Marquis Publishing
Herron Island, Washington
TwistedTourGuides.com

Vickers, Marques, 1957

TWISTED TOUR GUIDE TO LOS ANGELES
Shocking Deaths, Scandals and Vice

Dedication: To my daughters Charline and Caroline.

TABLE OF CONTENTS

PREFACE

4

ABOUT THE AUTHOR

SOURCES AND ARCHIVES SOURCED

Los Angeles Times, Los Angeles Herald Examiner, APNews.com, Daily News, DailyMail.co.uk, VCStar.com, New York Daily News, New York Times, San Francisco Chronicle, Huffpost.com, Wikipedia.org, FBI.gov, CrimeLibrary.com, Hoodline.com, OCWeekly.com, Murderpedia.com, Independent.com KCET.org, AtlasObscura.com, YouTube.com, About.com, California Department of Corrections and Rehabilitation Inmatelocator.cdcr.ca.gov, WoodTV.com, Pinterest.com, CityRating.com, InsideSoCal.com, CountryHomesOfAmerica.com, Websleuths.com, Edhat.com, AJC.com, CNN.com, CBSNews.com, Law.Justia.com, SFWeekly.com, Ssristories.org, ExiledOnline.com, CBSNews.com, KTLA.com, Keyt.com, TurnTo23.com, ODMP.org, Web.Archive.org, Cielodrive.com, Biography.com, Britannica.com, Heretical.com, FrontPageMag.com, SparselySageandTimely.com, LA.curbed.com, Chinarhyming.com, Homesteadmuseum.wordpress.com, OfficialColdCaseInvestigations.com, People Magazine, EvilBeings.com, LAWeekly.com, Murderfacts.com, Encyclopedia.com, Los Angeles Magazine, Good Housekeeping Magazine, SocietyofRock.com, Straightdope.com, Scpr.org,Caselaw, Findlaw.com, UPI.com, Rolling Stone Magazine, Psychology Today Magazine, AllThatsInteresting.com

Photography shot between 2016-2020. Some of the locations may have altered with time and ownership changes. Many of the locations are still privately inhabited. Please don't disturb the residents.

TWISTED TOUR GUIDE TO LOS ANGELES

Avoid The Tourist Herds.

What could be more uninspiring than seeing the identical attractions that everyone else has for decades?

This Twisted Tour Guide escorts you to the places locals don't want to talk about anymore...the same places people once couldn't stop talking about. Long after the screaming headlines and sensationalism has subsided, these bizarre, infamous and obscure historical sites remain hidden awaiting rediscovery.

Each visitation site in this guide is accompanied by a story. Many of the narratives defy believability, yet they are true. The profiled cast of characters feature saints and sinners (with emphasis towards the latter).

Notorious crimes, murders, accidental deaths, suicides, kidnappings, vice and scandal are captivating human interest tales. Paranormal activity in the aftermath is common.

The photography from each profile showcases the precise location where each event occurred. The scenes can seem ordinary, weird and sometimes very revealing towards clarifying the background behind events.

If you're seeking an alternative to conventional tourism, this Twisted Tourist Guide is ideal. Each directory accommodates the restless traveler and even resident looking for something unique and different. You will never imagine or scrutinize the City of Angels through rose tinted glasses again.

The Riches to Rags Fable of Pio Pico

Pico Boulevard is a major corridor that connects the core of mid-town Los Angeles with the Pacific Ocean in Westside Santa Monica. Its namesake, Pio Pico was a first generation Californian born in Mission San Gabriel in May 1801 to parents of Spanish, African and Native American ancestry.

After his father's death in 1819, Pico settled in San Diego, married in 1834 and by 1845 had immigrated to the Los Angeles settlement populated by 250 individuals where he briefly became governor. His tenure lasted twenty days, but was noteworthy for initiating the secularization process of the Spanish missions

As a leader in the California Assembly, he would be appointed governor again in 1845. He was outspoken in his preference towards California becoming a British Protectorate rather than an American territory.

During the Mexican-American War in 1846, U.S. Troops occupied Los Angeles and San Diego. Pico fled to Baja California but later returned to Los Angeles, a reluctant American citizen.

By the 1850s, Pico was considered one of the richest men in Alta (Upper) California. In 1850, he purchased the Rancho Paso de Bartolo that included half of the present day Whittier. Two years later, he constructed his home and ultimately resided there until 1892. His land holdings exceeded 500,000 acres stretching from the San Fernando Valley until portions of the current Camp Pendleton.

In 1868, Pico began construction of a three-story, 33-room hotel that he named the Pico House or *Casa de Pico*. Construction expense overruns prompted him to conduct

11

one of the worst real estate transactions imaginable. In exchange for $115,000 enabling his hotels' completion, Pico sold 60,000 acres of San Fernando Valley land that currently comprise the cities of Woodland Hills, Tarzana, Sherman Oaks, Van Nuys and North Hollywood.

The purchasing group known as the San Fernando Valley Farm Homestead Association was comprised of Issac Lankershim, Harris Newmark and several San Francisco based businessmen. Initially the Homestead group concentrated on raising 40,000 sheep on the property. When wool prices fell, they planted wheat. The grain transport trail that linked the San Fernando Valley to Santa Monica ultimately became Interstate 405.

Teaming with his son-in-law Isaac Newton Van Nuys, Lankershim cultivated the surest form of alchemy when they began subdividing lots for residential development at the turn of the century. With the completion of the Los Angeles Aqueduct bringing water from eastern California via the Owen Valley, the San Fernando Valley region exploded in growth and valuation.

Imagine…trading a hotel property for the richest slice of Valley real estate.

Pico completed his hotel in 1869. It was considered the finest and most lavish property in Southern California across from the old Los Angeles Plaza. As the surrounding neighborhood declined and commercial interests moved uptown, the property languished into a shabby house of prostitution. The hotel was deeded to the State of California in 1953 and is today used for occasional exhibits and special events.

The wealth of Pio Pico would dissipate through gambling,

further bad business practices, fraud, loansharking and the flood of 1883. He was forced to liquidate his real estate holdings and spent his final years in near poverty. He ended up living in his daughter's home where he died in 1894.

Aside from his poor business management and decision-making, Pico was renowned for his extreme ugliness. He was ridiculed for a disfigurement of his face. The cause was cited as a disease called *acromegaly*, not diagnosed until the late 19th century. The cause was an unregulated growth hormone, which ultimately distorts facial features by coarsening and exaggerating certain features.

In the words of prominent San Francisco writer Gertrude Atherton: *an uglier man than Pio Pico rarely had entered this world*.

Pico House
430 North Main Street, Los Angeles

PHOTO: Pico House

Calle de los Negroes and Hell's Half Acre

Los Angeles began to modernize during the latter half of the 19th Century with successive innovations including gaslights, electricity, passenger stagecoaches, trolley lines, railroads and more contemporary forms of entertainment.

Early 19th century local entertainment was dominated by a shuffling array of Mexican bands, religious plays, circuses, cockfights and bear fights. The animal engagements were staged at Chavez Ravine, the current home of Dodger Stadium.

Baser tastes would evolve into more refined preferences including classical music, opera and live dramatic theatre. Los Angeles was considered the secondary West Coast performance destination behind San Francisco.

In 1880, the population of the entire Los Angeles basin was a sparse 11,200, but the new decade would witness expansive growth pushing the population past 70,000 by 1888.

With this progressive growth, expansion and development spread uptown from the original El Pueblo Plaza core leaving a commercial abscess. The historical downtown territory beginning from the post-Civil War era featured block-long rows of adobe structures housing a mixture of reputable businesses, saloons, gambling halls and prostitute cribs. On the Plaza's eastern edge was an alley named *Calle de los Negros*. The Spanish used the term *Negro* to identify individuals of dark or black skin color. The context was not considered racially derogatory.

Los Angeles and particularly the *Calle de los Negros* quarter were renowned for violence and lawlessness. A

14

murder was reported daily in the district and most men strolled the streets armed with pistols and knives. Vigilante groups periodically stemmed the surge of violence, but often created further complications with their own excesses.

During the early evening of October 24, 1871, the notorious *Chinese Massacre* scarred the district caused by a local police office being caught in the crossfire between two rival Chinese gangs. The brutal vigilante reprisal resulted in nineteen Chinese men and boys being murdered. In 1877, *Calle de los Negros* was changed to *Los Angeles Street*. The conditions and squalor remained unchanged. Ten years later, the buildings along the former *Calle de los Negroes* were razed. Adobe constructions were replaced with fired brick masonry.

The modification enabled the already entrenched prostitution industry to flourish. The low-slung brick buildings featured diminutive pen-like rooms the approximate width of their front doors. These cubicles called *cribs* served as the working environment for hundreds of low-end prostitutes. Inside the cramped confines, sex workers often serviced a reported 13-30 men nightly with rates starting as low as one dollar per client.

The prostitutes posed on wooden platforms soliciting male patrons. Their fates were exploited by abusive pimps, clientele and exorbitant rents exacted by their landlords.

The Los Angeles crib district extended onto adjacent Alameda Street and achieved curiosity notoriety since the Southern Pacific Railroad tracks ran adjacent to Alameda. Passengers would pester train crews to forewarn them when approach to the red-light district was nearing.

Leading up to the 20th century, the district was called *Sonoratown* due to a significant population originating from the Mexican province of Sonoma. Many of the early Sonoratown residents immigrated as miners during the California gold rush. Segregation and racial hostilities prevented minorities from integrating into better neighborhoods uptown.

A significant contingent of Chinese settlers inhabited the quarter and segregated their brothels in the north end. The Chinese segment was ruled by secret societies called *Tongs* that governed the populace and prevented Anglo authority intervention through judicious bribery and law enforcement pay-offs. The majority of Chinese prostitutes were illegally imported through sex trafficking.

By the turn of the 20th century, Los Angeles' red-light district was christened *Hell's Half Acre* with the largest concentration of cribs confined within a triangular parcel originating at the juncture of Los Angeles and Alameda Streets.

Life for women working within this environment was dangerous and temporal. Suicide was common from opium overdoes. Sexually transmitted diseases and communicable diseases ravaged sex workers and clients indiscriminately.

Bartolo Ballerino dominated the crib trade owning a majority of the properties. Building titles were often registered under various women's names, but Ballerino ruthlessly controlled operations. Ballerino had grown up in Chile and arrived in California during the Gold Rush. He concentrated his Los Angeles real estate holdings within the Plaza core and cultivated local political influence.

Prostitution within Los Angeles was not illegal despite a

state law prohibiting the *renting out of rooms for immoral purposes*. In September 1903, Ballerino was arrested on Los Angeles Street for renting his property for the expressed purpose of prostitution. At trial, he fought the charges vigorously and the prosecuting attorney had great difficulty securing prostitutes willing to testify against their employer. Ballerino attempted to bribe a city clerk and many of his cribs were fenced in to keep out protesting Salvation Army members. His previous influence and law enforcement protection was rapidly slithering from his grasp.

In December 1903, the Los Angeles Police department raided the entire district chasing away and disbursing the hundreds who lived and worked there. The quarter went dark, but only temporarily.

Ballerino defiantly fought back elevating many of his ground floor cribs to the brilliantly lit second level of his centralized *International Hotel*. For two months his charade stimulated activity to the district. Upon his conviction in February 1904 and sentence of thirty days in jail, his reign was finished. Upon his release, his business had evaporated and he was consigned to living in one of the squalid and dingy rooms he once rented.

By the end of the decade, Ballerino was deceased and *Hell's Half Acre* obliterated. The entire district was eventually replaced by remnants of the 101 Freeway, wider roadways and the Union Station train garage. A new Chinatown district was officially christened in 1938 replacing the preceding *Little Italy* and *Sonoratown* sectors. The designation was primarily initiated to attract tourism. Motion picture set designers artificially staged the exotic oriental motifs, layout and statuary.

One of Ballerino's final published utterances before his death summed up the awkward evolution of the neighborhood. He declared emphatically: *This town is going to the dogs. It's getting too darned good.*

Calle de los Negroes and Hell's Half Acre:
Juncture of Los Angeles and Alameda Streets, Los Angeles

PHOTO: Park at the intersection of Los Angeles and Alameda Streets

The Slaying of Captain Walter Auble and Impressive Public Response

The respect and reverence that law enforcement once generated was profoundly evident with the public slaying of Los Angeles Police Captain Walter Auble during the daylight hours of September 9, 1908.

A beloved member of the Los Angeles police force for 23 years including a term as police-chief, Auble and his partner, Detective Paul Flammer were investigating a tip from a suspicious landlord about two potential burglary suspects, Carl Sutherland and Fred Horning. The policemen were admitted into an adjoining room where they overheard the suspect's casual conversation over their intent to commit a serious robbery within 48 hours. When the two suspects left their apartment, the police detectives discreetly searched their premises to confirm their suspicions.

A *Los Angeles Herald* newspaper article reported that they had found braces, jimmies, chisels, saws, electric flash lamps and keys of multiple varieties. In the bottom of a dressing case, under a pile of dirty clothes, two black masks, a blackjack, slingshot and two large sized revolvers were discovered. In the drawer of a table was a signed letter by Sutherland addressed to Horning advising him of their two major targeted addresses.

Attempting to thwart the imminent robbery, both officers dressed in plain-clothes and were escorted around the city. Auble sighted Sutherland and Horning strolling towards downtown from their eastbound passing car on Ninth Street. Their driver stopped the vehicle mid-block and let the two detectives out. They began following the men and but the pair suspected that they were being tailed. The two

19

suspects diverted their routing towards Grand Avenue.

Both bolted into a sprint but were overtaken by the two unarmed officers at the northeastern corner of North Grand and West Ninth Streets. Horning was seized and thrown headlong into a corner storefront carpet-beating establishment. He was arrested without further incident.

Sutherland responded to Captain Auble's demand to surrender by pulling out a long revolver from his coat pocket and firing directly into Auble's neck. As Auble crumpled to the ground he continued in an attempt to wrestle the gun away from the slightly built Sutherland. The suspect eventually fired three more shots amidst their struggle before Auble collapsed and released his grip on the weapon. He was taken to a nearby police receiving hospital where he died, despite emergency surgery from his wounds. It was reported that he shook hands with each of his surgeons personally and was surrounded by his family members when he expired.

Sutherland escaped immediate capture but the intensity and variety of his subsequent pursuit would be unimaginable today. An estimated 2,000 citizens participated in the manhunt via automobiles, on foot and on horseback following his trail of blood and random sightings. Officers from every department in the city and county donated their services.

Sutherland, who reportedly was habitually high on opiates, had the presence of mind to reload his gun at the intersection of Ninth and Hope Street. He sat down on the edge of the curbside, bound his bleeding left hand and then rolled and smoked a cigarette. He then penned a note, which he left lying on the spot swearing he would not be captured alive. He returned to his rooming house on

Georgia Street and exited with a single item before continuing his escape towards the Pacific Ocean via streetcar.

He had few options for escape. He was married but his wife was purportedly ignorant of his activities and true character. She was gainfully employed as an operator by the Home Telephone Company of Long Beach and well regarded.

Sutherland was sighted definitively near Redondo Street. Several bloodhounds were borrowed to resume the chase. Police were advised that he would likely seek sanctuary at an acquaintance's house that evening on South Broadway Street near the present day intersection of 77th Street, then an isolated and lonely country road. The acquaintance worked with Sutherland as a waiter at both the California and University Clubs.

Sutherland walked into the stakeout twelve hours after the shooting and was arrested without resistance. He appeared anemic and casually tossed his revolver to the ground. He raised his right hand above his head. With his left hand, he deftly inserted a small bottle into his lips and swallowed the contents.

The liquid cyanide he had retrieved from his rooming house almost immediately contracted his muscles once the handcuffs were attached. Despite frenzied respiration techniques by the arresting officers, he slipped silently into death inside a patrol car that was rushing him to the same hospital as Auble.

Captain Auble was considered a model and universally popular officer, particularly within ethnic communities. A bizarre request for his killer Sutherland's cadaver was made by members of a Chinatown merchants committee and later published. The delegation wished to boil Sutherland's body in a preparation of acids, then heap abuse upon it and throw it out on a refuse heap where it could rot in the sun with none of the sacred Chinese emblems employed to drive away evil spirits.

The request was denied as his grieving wife was allowed to make burial arrangements. The outrage and sorrow felt by the community and press was genuine. Only a half-century earlier, Los Angeles was a disbursed settlement of intolerance, intemperance and lawlessness defined by enormous sprawling rancheros and a small concentrated city base. Vigilantes loosely supplanted established law enforcement and governed the unmanageable anarchy.

The frontier era had passed and Los Angeles had evolved into an expanding urban center of 300,000 by 1910. Within the following ten years, the population would double following a post-World War I boom.

Fred Horning was originally charged with murder. Those charges were dropped but he was still sentenced to fourteen years at Folsom Prison where he had recently been imprisoned. Following his subsequent release, his name would disappear from public archives.

Today, the corner of West Ninth and South Grand Streets is undergoing yet another transformation. The storefront and sidewalk where Auble was shot are a vacant lot under excavation. A church adjacent north of the site on Grand Avenue at the time of the killing was razed to be replaced in the 1920s by a 9-story office building. This structure is currently in the stages of further renovation or demolition.

Reminders of Los Angeles' architectural past today are

often given historical protection status. With the steady evolution of downtown vertical development, planning boards have attempted to maintain equilibrium between legacy and progress. This philosophy is in direct contrast with mid-20th century haste that leveled first and built indiscriminately afterwards.

Captain Walter Auble's death has become a casualty consigned to obscure memorial plaques and records. The cooperative and enthusiastic public involvement involved with his killer's capture proved an insightful contrast to contemporary attitudes and apathy towards law enforcement. The tragedy behind his death is only equaled by the tragedy of the public and media's eroded faith and trust.

Captain Walter Auble's Murder Site:
Corner West Ninth and Grand Avenue, Los Angeles

PHOTO: Murder site:

The *Los Angeles Times* Headquarters Firebombing

The *Los Angeles Times'* fourth headquarters formerly encompassed West First Street to the north, South Spring Street to the east, West Second Street to the south and Broadway Street to the west. Gordon B. Kaufmann designed the initial building, an art deco construction, which opened in 1935. The parcel, named Times Mirror Square later added four additional buildings to the site. Facing South Broadway Street, the existing structures are used principally for offices, parking and filming locations.

The site on the corner of South Spring and West First Streets was previously the Hotel Nadeau until its demolition in 1932. Extending on South Spring to West Second Street was formerly the Culver Block building on the southeastern corner, used as City Hall between 1884-1888.

The *Times* was first published in 1881 as the *Los Angeles Daily Times*. When the original founders ran into financial difficulties, the paper was foreclosed to its printer, the Mirror Printing Office and Book Bindery. Harrison Gray Otis was hired as the editor and astutely turned the newspaper into a financial success. Within three years, he and Colonel H. H. Boyce purchased the entire organization. Otis later bought out his partner's interest. In 1886, the term *Daily* was removed from the masthead.

The *Times'* initial headquarters was a small brick *Times* building located on the corner of Temple and New High Streets. The second *Times* three-story building would be constructed in 1886 on the southwestern corner of West First and South Broadway Streets adjacent to the present site. Next-door in a 1905 photograph was a store named the Ark and American Café with a boarding house located above.

In 1910, a dynamite charge exploded outside of the building and nearby gas lines sparking a catastrophic fire. Two employees died in the telegraph room, sixteen in the linotype and composing room and eight bodies were found at the bottom of a freight elevator shaft. The *Times* was renowned for its fiery anti-union rhetoric. The paper continued printing from an auxiliary press located at 531 South Spring, now a parking lot adjacent to the Spring Arcade Building.

Two disgruntled union officials, James and John McNamara, detonated the explosives. The union hired famed attorney Clarence Darrow to represent the brothers. Darrow convinced the brothers to plead guilty to avoid the death penalty and was indicted himself for jury tampering by attempting to bribe a juror.

The judge rejected a plea bargain deal offered by the prosecutor and John McNamara was sentenced to life in prison at San Quentin where he died in 1941. James was sentenced to fifteen years, which he served at Folsom and San Quentin prisons. He died two months before his brother while still incarcerated. Darrow was acquitted on the charge of bribery but was rumored to have accepted a deal forcing him to leave town and promise to never practice law in California again. His most famous trials were yet to come including the Leopold and Loeb, Ossian Street and John T. Scopes *Monkey Trial*, a pivotal national drama over the teaching of Darwin's Theory of Evolution in public school classrooms.

The *Times* became Los Angeles' dominant newspaper with the decline of the *Herald Examiner* during the latter 1960s and 70s. They remained the sole daily general circulation newspaper based downtown until 2018.

The Los Angeles Times is no longer locally owned. The newspaper was acquired in 2000 by the Tribune Company, which also published the *Chicago Tribune* and *Baltimore Sun*. In April 2018, the newspaper relocated their operations to El Segundo after failing to arrive at suitable terms upon the expiration of their lease.

Former Los Angeles Times Headquarters:
Times Mirror Square, Los Angeles

PHOTO: Los Angeles Times Building Facade

Pasadena's Infamous Suicide Bridge

The elevated Colorado Street Bridge was opened in 1913 to replace the diminutive Scoville Bridge located below crossing the Arroyo Seco River. The span is located on the western periphery of Pasadena connecting with Eagle Rock. Shortly after its completion, the Scoville Bridge was washed away by rare floodwaters. The Colorado Street span is designed with distinctive Beaux Arts arches, light standard and railings, the span aesthetically curves so that the design footings are strategically situated on more solid ground. The bridge is 1,486 feet long and raises a maximum of 150 feet at its highest apex.

Locals rarely call the structure by its official name. Instead it has been labeled *Suicide Bridge* for tangible reasons since it's opening. During construction, a worker fell to his death and landed in the wet concrete under the bridge. His accidental plunge was followed by dozens of desperate individuals terminating their lives from deliberate jumps. A surge in fatalities occurred during the Great Depression.

One of the most repeated suicide related stories involved a mother who tossed her infant off the bridge and then followed with her own leap. The mother plummeted to her death, but the child landed in a tree unharmed.

Suicide barrier fences have been erected to discourage jumpers. Although credited with preventing some impulsive leaps, every year more fatalities add to the chilling tally. The bridge has been depicted and filmed in numerous movie and television programs along with music videos, but *never* as a sanctioned source for final departure.

Colorado Street Bridge
504 W Colorado Boulevard, Pasadena

PHOTO: Colorado Street Bridge

Family Skeletons Buried Amidst a Historic Craftsman Estate

The Lanterman House is an impressionably understated La Canada Flintridge Arts and Crafts bungalow constructed in 1915. The landmark remains one of the communities few surviving pre-1920 residences. It was nicknamed *El Refugio* by its original owners Roy and Emily Lanterman.

Patriarch Jacob Lanterman and his wife Amoretta immigrated to Southern California from East Lansing, Michigan in the 1870s. They sought a more accommodating climate. Jacob and another midwestern pioneer combined to purchase 5,835 acres of barren and arid landscape absent of water rights.

Their initial construction became an estate called *Homewood* on Verdugo Road that became the rural social center. Water rights remained an elusive detriment to growth. The closest and most convenient source was a stream located in Pickens Canyon. Negotiations for water access with owner Theodor Pickens stalled endlessly. Amoretta allegedly decided to expedite the process. She rode out to the Pickens homestead armed with a shotgun and indicated neither she nor the weapon would be departing until a resolution was formalized. Pickens agreed to her terms.

The Lanterman's son Roy studied at the University of Maryland and John Hopkins University earning his medical degree. In 1893, he returned to Southern California and began an obstetrical practice in Los Angeles. He established residence in Santa Monica where he met his future socially ambitious and cultured wife Emily. His medical practice flourished. The couple soon had two sons to complete traditional family expectations.

Roy made his first tactical error when he ran for the office of Los Angeles County Coroner in 1906. A conservative Republican, he won and upon his swearing in, pushed expediently for radical reforms...too fast for the comfort level of some party members. He established the first county morgue and attempted to increase his staff size.

In January 1907, an unsuccessful lawsuit to remove him from office was launched based on a claim of election fraud. On December 18th, the *Los Angeles Times* reported his arrest for intoxication, battery and creating a disturbance at a local house of prostitution. He was arrested armed with two revolvers and concluded the evening in the county drunk tank.

Public indignation immediately demanded his resignation. Lanterman claimed the episode was a *set up* and hired a reputable lawyer to represent him. Charges against him were dropped, but he resigned on January 27, 1908.

His ordeal was not complete. His adversaries weren't satisfied with a simple public humiliation. On the day of his resignation, a secret grand jury issued an arrest warrant charging him with *having sworn to false statements* regarding his election expenses.

His father Jacob was dying when he was put on trial. He was convicted of defrauding the county and sentenced to a year in prison at San Quentin. His wife emerged as his primary public advocate, pleading pathetically for a new trial or simply probation to seemingly unreceptive public officials.

Roy Lanterman's lawyers appealed the verdict and

apparently were successful. He returned to his successful private practice and his wife regained her social status. In 1915 against her wishes, he decided to return home to pastoral La Canada. The couple hired architect Arthur Haley to design their mansion on 35 acres of family property. Concrete was employed to make the structure more earthquake resistant and sunlight-attracting features were integrated to enhance the presence of natural light.

The hoped-for refuge from urban pressures and stress proved temporary. In 1916, Roy was served with an arrest warrant for performing an illegal abortion on a 17-year-old. The California Medical Board was in the midst of a statewide crusade to prohibit medically performed abortions. He was detained for 24 hours in the county jail then released on a legal technically.

The scandal briefly cost him his license to practice medicine. He was arrested again in 1917 for murder following a woman's death from a botched abortion. At trial, he was found *not guilty* because the unfortunate victim had confided to several people that she had performed the abortion on herself.

His troubles were not complete when in 1918 he was accused of *contributing to the delinquency of a minor.* The claimant, a 19 year-old stenographer claimed that he had seduced her into an affair while she worked at the family home. He denied the charges and the outcome of the case was never publicly disclosed.

His final trial occurred in 1929 when he and another doctor were charged with the murder of a dancer. He was once again acquitted when a corroborated story confirmed that his sole role was late and futile assistance after she'd performed her own abortion with tragic results.

Emily Lanterman remained with him throughout each adversity and scandal. Roy continued his practice uneventfully in town and out of his house for the next twenty years. The couple quietly raised their sons who followed divergent paths. One served notably in state politics and the other remained at *El Refugio* cultivating a passion for organ music and performance. Neither ever married.

Roy Lanterman died in 1947 and Emily the following year. His obituary omitted his previous scandals. Their sons died in 1981 and 1987 and ownership of the property was deeded over to the city of La Canada-Flintridge ironically founded by their grandfather over a century previously.

Lanterman House:
4420 Encinas Drive, La Canada Flintridge

PHOTO: Lanterman House

The Resolute Will To Keep William Desmond Taylor's Murder Unsolved

William Desmond Taylor was discovered on the morning of February 2, 1922 dead inside his bungalow at the Alvarado Court Apartments in the trendy Westlake Park district of downtown Los Angeles. In his pocket was a wallet holding $78 in cash, a silver cigarette case, pocket watch, penknife and locket bearing the photograph of actress Mabel Normand. A two-carat diamond ring remained on his finger.

Missing was an undisclosed large amount of cash he had shown to his accountant the day before, a motive and ultimately an incentive by police to resolve the mystery.

The original officiating doctor indicated that Taylor had died of a stomach hemorrhage. When police investigators rolled the body over, it became obvious that Taylor had been fatally shot in the back at least once. The doctor's identity was never revealed and he was never heard from again.

Between 1914-1922, Taylor acted in 27 and directed 59 silent films. The film industry was exploding and money following. Prosperity proliferated but shadows were darkening the horizon. The year previously, Roscoe Fatty Arbuckle had been accused of murder and moral degradation involving the death of actress Virginia Rapp.

The scandalous murder of Taylor, widely respected within the industry, threatened to crumble the fragile golden pillars of lucrative commerce. There remained only one prudent course of action: inaction. The *City Hall Gang* controlled Los Angeles' municipal government and a scaled down investigation or silence could be assured by graft.

National newspapers found murder investigation an inventive sport. Numerous suspects emerged convictable in print. All seemingly had murderous motives. None were arrested.

The suspects included: Edward Sands (Taylor's former valet and a former convict), Henry Peavey (Taylor's current valet who found the body and another former convict), Mabel Normand (a love interest who Taylor attempted to cure of cocaine addiction), Charles Eyton (General Manager of Paramount Pictures seen removing compromising items from Taylor's bungalow), Mary Miles Minter (an underage actress and sexual liaison), Charlotte Shelby (Minter's mother), Ross Sheridan (a reputed blackmailer) and Margaret Gibson (never an official suspect but she confessed to the murder on her 1964 deathbed).

A neighbor, Faith Cole MacLean claimed to have viewed an intruder who appeared in costume and was possibly a woman disguised as a man. Numerous subsequent publications speculated wildly on the puzzling case that refused to be solved.

Taylor was reputedly raised from Anglo-Irish gentry. His polish and manners endeared him to the industry elite. He entered the armed forces as a private at the age of 46 to fight in World War I. By the time he arrived in France ready for combat, the conflict was completed. He was ultimately promoted to the temporary grade of lieutenant before he was discharged.

His death provoked shock amongst the film colony. His former four-year fiancé, Neva Gerber typified him as the soul of honour, a man of personal culture, education and refinement.

None of these endearing qualities prevented his killing.

The Alvarado Court bungalows were long ago leveled to accommodate a small retail shipping center parking lot. The downtown Los Angeles film colony relocated to Hollywood and then dispersed globally. Mabel Normand's scandals and tuberculosis forced an early retirement from films and premature death at only 37 in 1930.

In 1924, her own chauffeur would shoot to death millionaire oil broker Courtland S. Dines with her pistol. Dines was romantically involved with Normand's friend and Taylor's other next-door neighbor Edna Purviance. Normand was the last person to reportedly see Taylor alive and wept inconsolably throughout his funeral ceremony.

For all that William Desmond Taylor appeared to be missed. It seemed equally desirable for his killer to remain unknown.

William Desmond Taylor's Bungalow:
404B South Alvarado Street, Los Angeles (Since demolished)

PHOTO:
Former site of the Alvarado Court bungalows

The Valhalla Memorial Cemetery Scam: Preying on the Living

The Portal of the Folded Wings is a monumental gateway originally designating the entrance to Burbank's Valhalla Memorial Cemetery. Construction began in mid-1924, designed in the *Spanish Mission Revival* style by local architect Kenneth McDonald. Elaborate statuary and decorative moldings were fashioned by sculptor Federico Giorgi who was responsible for the massive Babylonian elephants and lions showcased in the film *Intolerance*.

The ornamental edifice became the crowning centerpiece in a real estate swindle that marketed burial plots with the same aggressive and ethical scruples as Florida swampland.

In March 1923, John R. Osborne and C. C. Fitzpatrick established a corporation headquartered in downtown Los Angeles. Using investor's funds, they purchased 65 acres of flatlands amidst the rural dairy farms and stockyards of Burbank. Access to the property was only reachable via an extended dirt road. The nearest mortuary within the Los Angeles basin was over an hour and a half away.

An elaborate cemetery was planned for the property and christened *Valhalla*, which in Nordic mythology represented an enormous heavenly gallery inhabited by brave warriors and gods. Within a year, hundreds of salesmen were employed to promote the purchase of burial plots as an infallible investment. Targeting unsophisticated investors, the ruse quickly generated enough funds to purchase an adjacent 52-acres designated to host a Mausoleum Park.

Osborne's credibility stemmed erroneously from his

assurances that he was an experienced graveyard manager. The employed sales pitch was based on the projected explosive growth of the Los Angeles basin (accurate). More dubious was their assertion that the primary motivation behind the expansion was the ill health and advanced age of the incoming residents. Marketers stressed a severe Los Angeles shortage of burial grounds and the city's refusal to add additional cemeteries. Their most outrageous claim stemmed from their declarations that bodies were currently being buried atop each other in 3-foot graves instead of the traditional six. The salesmen reasoned that flipping these investment plots would certainly generate rapid and significant profits as burial space became scarcer.

The elemental flaw in their scheme was that no shortage existed. Los Angeles' cemeteries were ably capable of accommodating one million additional burials. At Valhalla, multiple deeds were sold and issued for identically located plots. For approximately a year, the campaign brought in substantial income, estimated between $3-4 million. Suspicious salesmen regarding the accuracy of their claims and company management practices were immediately terminated. The isolation of the Burbank property made investor visits impractical and infrequent.

By the beginning of 1924, hundreds of the estimated four thousand buyers began to organize and mobilize. They sent letters en mass to the local Real Estate Commissioner and staged large protest meetings. Many had fallen behind in their payments and were in jeopardy of losing title. Some had simply had exhausted their meager savings anticipating a quick turnover that never materialized.

In December 1924, the federal government intervened charging Osborne, Fitzpatrick and four others with illegally using the postal service to defraud with their project's promotion. In August 1925, Osborne and Fitzpatrick were found guilty and sentenced to ten years and ten days in a federal penitentiary. The duo immediately filed a series of appeals enabling their temporary freedom on bail. With their financial gains still intact, a preposterous story became even stranger.

John R. Osborne hired a personable automobile salesman named Jack Gordon to serve as his valet and traveling companion. In November, the pair were staying at the Maryland Hotel in Pasadena. Osborne reportedly entered the bathroom to shave. When he returned to the room, he discovered $103,000 in liberty bonds and $800 in cash missing. Gordon had mysteriously vanished. Osborne reported the theft to police.

Gordon had not only stolen the proceeds but had lied about his identity. He was actually a wanted Chicago based gunman and professional crook named Harold Whittaker operating under multiple alias. He was able to convert the bonds into cash with the assistance of his girlfriend and proceeded to squander the money leaving an easily traceable trail. He was arrested in Cleveland during January 1926 and returned to Los Angeles. He escaped three months later but was once again arrested in New York that November after robbing a dance hall. This time he was expediently escorted to prison.

In March 1925, *The Portal of the Folded Wings* was officially dedicated and an accompanying public concert was staged. Burial ceremonies had already begun and the facility began to resemble a sustainable operation.

Appeals exhausted, Osborne and Fitzpatrick entered Leavenworth Federal Prison to serve their sentence in June 1927. While incarcerated, Osborne became acquainted with former USC football legend George Meadows who was serving a term for selling stolen liberty bonds. This prison association would prove costly.

Osborne's father, John E., assumed management of the cemetery, taking no salary and publicly stated his intention to pay back investors his misguided son had defrauded. He was perhaps the sole conscientious individual amidst this entire sordid escapade.

George Meadows was released from Leavenworth and immediately headed to Burbank and an appointment with Osborne Sr. He boasted of having ties to local prominent attorneys and officials in Washington D.C. that insured his ability to intervene on behalf of Osborne's son. Meadows outrageously claimed to have met with President Calvin Coolidge to discuss viable options. The gullible Osborn Sr. paid him $23,000 assuming the funds would be deployed towards attorneys and officials to obtain a pardon or parole.

Osborne was mistaken. The devious but not particularly brilliant Meadows was arrested shortly afterwards. He returned to prison after being convicted on eleven counts of grand theft. His nickname of *Malicious Meadows* had been well cultivated during his university years.

Osborne and Fitzpatrick were released from Leavenworth in 1930 after serving only three years of their sentence. Both returned to Valhalla Park leadership positions joining Osborne, Sr. In their absence, Burbank had changed substantially.

The community became the center of West Coast aviation hosting numerous aerospace companies and an airport called Angeles Mesa Drive adjacent to the cemetery. Lockheed Corporation arrived in the 1930s and purchased the airport, renaming it the Lockheed Air Terminal. *The Portal of the Folded Wings* evolved into a popular location for public concerts and live radio broadcasts. The cemetery was now a fully functional operation and became the burial site for numerous high-profile local residents and celebrities from the entertainment industry.

A fairy tale ending became illusionary. With the instigators of the original fraud back in management, stockholders became wary of disappearing assets. Four lot holders demanded the appointment of a receivership to assume control of the park. Management responded in 1932 by filing multiple lawsuits for slander.

In September 1935, John E. Osborne Sr. was summoned to an unspecified downtown Los Angeles business meeting. He never appeared. Instead, he fired a bullet into his heart in his garage killing himself instantly. He was buried within Valhalla. The Osborne-Fitzpatrick management team eventually was forced to sell the cemetery to the state.

John R. Osborne shifted occupations but not scruples or stripes. He became a bookmaker for a large gambling establishment near Santa Monica Boulevard and La Brea Avenue. He turned state's witness in 1941 under the protection of immunity.

In 1950, Pierce Brothers purchased Valhalla Memorial Park. They added a new administration building, mortuary chapel and three new mausoleums. They relocated the main entrance to Victory Boulevard in North Hollywood leaving *The Portal of the Folded Wings* as orphaned statuary serving decorative, but no functional purpose.

During the 1950's the focus of the memorial was shifted into a shrine honoring aviation. Periodic ceremonies and bronze plaques honored prominent pioneers and distinctive aerospace achievements.

In July 1969 a small twin-engine airplane taking off from the Lockheed Airport crashed into the Portal's dome killing the pilot and one passenger. The dome was subsequently repaired.

In the late 1970s, the neighboring cities of Burbank, Glendale and Pasadena purchased the airport from Lockheed. The company would relocate their headquarters during the following decade. The airport was named after Bob Hope in 2003 in homage to the late comedian and nearby Toluca Lake resident.

Few remain alive who can remember the Valhalla Park plot swindle. Even fewer can likely conceive why buying Burbank burial grounds ever seemed like a sage and alluring real estate investment.

Valhalla Memorial Park
10621 Victory Boulevard, North Hollywood

The Julian Oil Company Scandal: Prelude to the Global Market Crash

During a downtown real estate bust period of 1890, the Los Angeles City Oil Field was discovered stretching immediately south of Chavez Ravine westward to Vermont Avenue. The underground source encompassed a territory of approximately four miles in length by a quarter mile in width. Fortunes and major exploration wells created a decade long oil boom. The success of tapping this vein led to further drillings within the Los Angeles Basin. During the peak year of 1901, approximately 200 separate oil companies were actively exploiting the downtown field. Today dense residential and commercial development has been constructed above the reserves.

No individual profited from the boom period shrewder than a piano teacher from Kentucky named Emma Summers. Starting with a half-interest investment in a well she'd purchased from her piano lessons, she parlayed success upon success. Each lucrative drill enabled her to acquire additional operations, ultimately forcing many of her competitors out of business. A self-sufficient woman, Summers did her own accounting and despite her wealth, continued to offer piano lessons in the evening. At the peak of drilling prosperity, she controlled nearly half of the wells amidst the center sector of the field.

At the furthest northern extremity of Spring Street above Chinatown is an area that once boasted a horizon of pumping derricks. This territory today encompasses the Los Angeles State Historic Park and Cathedral High School. The concentration of drilling extended along the present Pasadena Freeway, snaking along the routing of Third Street until the intersection of Vermont Avenue. The daily nonstop pumping nearly depleted the oil reservoirs. Price ultimately flattened the boom from a peak of $1.80 a barrel in 1901 to 15¢ a barrel in 1903 due to overproduction and increased competition from San Joaquin Valley based operations.

Although local resources were no longer tapped so vigorously, a subsequent regional petroleum boom resurfaced during the 1920's. The concept of creating instant wealth never loses its appeal.

In 1922, Canadian citizen Courtney Chauncey (C.C.) Julian arrived in California claiming expertise and vast experience in property speculation and oil exploration. He immediately secured drilling rights to five acres in Santa Fe Springs. He recruited investors through splashy ads in the *Los Angeles Times*. His marketing expertise was grounded in convincing speculators, gamblers and small-scale investors that his shrewd and infallible oil field selection would soon supplant the dominant Standard Oil Company. He claimed to have discovered the deepest well in Southern California.

The following year, he incorporated the Julian Petroleum Company and within a frenzied two months had sold $5 million worth of stock in his designated drilling operation, Julian Pete. His company had been authorized to issue 159,000 shares of preferred stock, but an estimated 4-5 million shares reportedly circulated.

The vehicle he employed to create credibility was a parallel scheme fueled by a small band of wealthy investors. This insider group purchased enormous blocks of Julian stock artificially and rapidly inflating values. Observers of this hyper growth were easily attracted and seduced into becoming new investors. Celebrity investment banker Motley Flint whose status and connections were revered by the Los Angeles financial and film industry elite headed this insider faction called the *Million Dollar Pool*.

Towards the end of 1924, C.C. Julian discreetly sold his interest in his namesake oil company to Sheridan C. Lewis.

Rather than skip town, he continued to dabble and speculate during the next few years in lead mining ventures and stock marketing schemes. He maintained a high-profile presence in the Los Angeles social and nightclub scene. He spent liberally and confidently averting suspicion away from the teetering structure supporting his bogus financial mirage.

The inevitable collapse of the Julian Petroleum Company occurred without warming in May 1927. California regulators and the Los Angeles Stock Exchange revoked the company's stock-selling permit due to their flagrant violation of over issuing shares.

Although no longer officially affiliated with the organization, C. C. Julian attempted to explain and rationalize the collapse via a radio broadcast on his own station KMTR. A competition radio station reportedly tampered with the broadcast by drowning out his voice with shrieks and howls whenever he attempted to speak. Present Julian Petroleum owner Sheridan Lewis pledged a massive reorganization of the company along with an explanation as to why growth soured. Nothing was forthcoming. He resigned and declared bankruptcy soon afterwards.

Over forty thousand investors experienced their savings and investments evaporate. The fraud exceeded $150 million. The scenario would be repeated with the New York Stock Exchange collapse two years later.

As lawsuits accumulated and scheduled court dates became the new business agenda, the fate of two principals concluded in separate but equal catastrophe.

On July 14, 1930, financial savant and former officer of the First National Bank Motley Flint was testifying in a civil trial between David O. Selznick and his former bank. Flint took the stand under oath attempting vainly to recall details regarding a loan transaction between the two parties.

Flint's stature had been tarnished by his insider role in the Julian Petroleum collapse, but still carried clout. He was a Master Mason within California, his brother was a U.S. Senator and he maintained some loyal allies. Jack and Sam Warner publicly espoused that without Flint's previous moral and financial support, their studio would have never materialized.

Flint completed his testimony and proceeded towards the spectator section. Frank Keaton, a disgruntled Julian investor who'd lost his entire life savings rose from the second row and fired three shots pointedly at Flint. The first struck Flint's neck, the second punctured his heart and the third his lung and liver. Flint collapsed dying instantly. Keaton tossed the .38 Smith and Wesson revolver on the corpse and collapsed back into his seat wailing inconsolably. The presiding judge raced from behind his bench and to immobilize him.

C. C. Julian endured no such immediate retribution. He wisely skipped Los Angeles for Oklahoma and attempted to resuscitate varying financial frauds. His good fortune began to wane, but he still possessed financial resources and arrogance. In March 1933, he masqueraded as an impoverished Irish citizen with a false passport and boarded a steamer from Seattle. His destination was

Shanghai and another attempt at reinvention.

Profiting from Shanghai's lax entry regulations, Julian shed his disguise upon arrival. American authorities attempted to extradite him, but being a Canadian national made the process problematic.

Julian established residence initially at the respectable Astor Hotel and subsequently the upscale Metropole, resuming an opulent lifestyle. The charade withered within nine months. His cons and schemes failed to materialize in Shanghai and he himself was frequently victimized. The Metropole evicted him from his lodgings once his illicit finances were drained. His drinking and ultimate alcoholism deteriorated his former charm.

He borrowed a significant sum of money from a local businessman. He never repaid the debt. During the next unproductive year, he relocated lodgings to the marginal Frenchtown Hotel. His enterprises failed and cruel reality finally terminated his ambitions. He decided to conclude his despicable existence with a final flourish. He checked into the Astor Hotel with a companion, a local stenographer named Leonora Levy, feasted on a lavish dinner and swallowed poison in his sumptuous room accompanied with champagne.

Five hours later he expired. Levy finished the poison and lapsed into a coma. She survived. She attended his funeral attended by eight others. She mourned his death in white as was the Chinese custom, followed the procession and remained briefly by his graveside weeping. She then returned to her daytime job, lacking any other alternative.

C.C. Julian and Motley Flint's legacies would subsequently remain as forgotten as their cursed stock swindle.

Julian Petroleum Company Headquarters
Pershing Square Building
448 South Hill Street, Ninth Floor, Los Angeles

PHOTO: Pershing Square Office Building

Cecil Hotel: Expedient Check-Ins and Permanent Check-Outs

The Cecil Hotel opened in 1927 intended for international businessmen and Los Angeles social elites. The property's Beaux-arts design features a marble lobby, stained-glass windows, palm trees and a decorative staircase. The intended deluxe property faced almost immediate financial challenges with the start of the Great Depression two years later and encroaching Skid Row district, inhabited by a homeless and vagrant population.

The reputation of the neighborhood soon infiltrated into the Cecil attracting unsavory guests and tenants. The property also cultivated an additional reputation as a *terminal* destination point. During the 1930s, six reported suicides involved ingested poisonings, slit throats and self-inflicted gunshot wounds. Over the subsequent years, the majority of suicides involved simply jumping from upper level rooms. One of the most bizarre occurred in 1962 when an estranged spouse jumped from the ninth floor and landed on a pedestrian below killing them both.

Three of the most infamous guests have included serial killers Richard *The Night Stalker* Ramirez, Jack Unterweger and mutilation victim Elizabeth *Black Dahlia* Short. Ramirez committed several of his murders within nearby Los Angeles areas while living in a room on the top floor. He reportedly discarded his bloody clothing into the hotel's dumpster following his killings. Austrian born Unterweger selected the hotel due to Ramirez's notoriety and targeted local prostitutes, strangling them with their bras. Short stayed at the property days before her grisly murder which remained unsolved.

The accompanying violence and mystery has resulted in the

Cecil Hotel being labeled as a *haunted* destination. New owners in 2011 changed the name of the property, but couldn't fully eradicate the sequence of strange occurrences.

In 2013, a Canadian college student was discovered dead inside a water tank on the roof of the hotel three weeks after she'd been announced missing. Her naked cadaver was found after hotel guests complained of faulty water pressure and a funny taste to the hotel's water. Her death was ironically ruled as an *accidental drowning*. Prior to her death, surveillance cameras observed her behaving strangely in an elevator, yelling at someone out of viewsight and waving her arms erratically.

Was she batting away the macabre and uninvited evil spirits accompanying her stay?

Hotel Cecil (Currently Stay on Main Hotel and Hostel)
640 South Main Street, Los Angeles

PHOTO: Hotel Cecil

Sister Aimee Floods The Masses With Her Spiritual Urgency

Flamboyant television evangelical preachers owe a significant debt to Aimee Semple McPherson for laying the groundwork on how to manipulate mass media for exposure purposes generating both funding and expansive growth. Known during her era as *Sister Aimee*, television was not yet available, but she cultivated the fertile recruiting potential of radio, film, theatre and musicals to preach her message often accompanied by public faith healing demonstrations. Her weekly sermons and theatrical stagings from the Angelus Temple created one of the first megachurches. She is credited with the founding the Foursquare Gospel Church.

At the peak of her popularity during the 1920s, she gave up to 22 sermons weekly with her lavish Sunday evening service attracting overflowing crowds. Her Angelus Temple, completed in 1923, along with her other ambitious projects were financed by offering collections taken at every meeting. One of her more unintentionally humorous admonishments during the offering was *no coins please!*

Her extraordinary popularity seemed improbable given her humble upbringing. She was born and raised in a rural Ontario, Canada farmhouse. Her initial exposure to religion came in the form of her mother's work with the poor in Salvation Army soup kitchens.

During a revival meeting, she met Robert Semple, a Pentecostal missionary from Ireland. She was so enamored by Semple and his preaching that she married him in 1908 and accompanied him to China as a missionary. Both contracted malaria and he died of dysentery in Hong Kong. Following her recovery, she gave birth to their daughter and returned to New York City, a 19-year-old widow to work with her mother at the Salvation Army.

She remarried in 1913 and had another son with an accountant Harold McPherson. They relocated to Providence, Rhode Island. She felt a strong emotional call to begin preaching prompted by a *persistent voice* that she finally couldn't ignore. In 1915, she impulsively abandoned her husband and departed with her two children beginning on a pilgrimage of tented revival meetings. He joined her weeks later and they sold their Providence home. His enthusiasm waned when he realized the uncertainty of a vagabond life absent of financial security and stability. They officially separated in 1918 and divorced three years later.

Semple's charismatic preaching and magnetic personality relocated her destiny to a stable base on the West Coast. The endless traveling and touring wearied her. Her focused energy and fundraising created a movement ideal for the expanding Los Angeles basin and national radio audience. She mobilized her operations into charity work, food kitchens and humanitarian aid.

Her preaching philosophy was conservative with a strong emphasis against the theory of evolution. She accentuated the power of speaking in tongues and healings. Extravagant theatrical backdrops and costuming frequently dressed her presentations. She had a propensity to christen slogans including the *Heavenly Airplane*, *Amen Corner*, *Hallelujah Chorus*, *Gospel Car*, etc. still employed by today's evangelists. She was active politically, but vague on her political party leanings. She steadfastly reinforced her belief that America was founded and sustained by divine inspiration.

By 1925, she was considered one of the most influential women and ministers of her era. She became a celebrity equal to any entertainment, sports or political figure. She liked to portray her image as someone an adoring public could embrace *without compromising their souls*. The success of her Los Angeles operations permitted her to tour the United States via airplane or rail and resume her regional revival crusades.

The impeccable character of Sister Aimee suffered its first blemish when on May 18, 1926, she mysteriously disappeared from Ocean Park Beach in Santa Monica. Fearful she had likely drowned, divers searched the waters and volunteers combed the beach and nearby areas for evidence or clues of her whereabouts. Over the succeeding weeks, Aimee sightings were phoned in from all over the United States. Some of the hoax calls audaciously demanded ransom. Over a month passed and the Angelus Temple began preparing her memorial service presuming she was deceased.

On June 23rd, her mother received a phone call from Douglas, Arizona indicating that her daughter was alive and rehabilitating in a local hospital. What emerged was an incredulous story of Aimee being abducted by a couple at the beach who'd asked her to pray over their sick child. She was shoved into a car, forced to inhale a drug-laced cloth rendering her unconscious and eventually transported to a small shack in the Mexican desert.

Her dramatic escape began via a window while her captors were away on errands. She then trekked 13 miles through inhospitable desert before reaching a Mexican border town named Agua Prieta. She was transported by locals to Douglas following her collapse from exhaustion. A turnout estimated between 30,000 to 50,000 welcomed the heroine's return to Los Angeles.

Not everyone was moved much less believed Sister Aimee's ordeal. Rumors circulated that her entire disappearance was faked. The Los Angeles Attorney General forwarded a more plausible theory publicly. His speculation was that Sister Aimee had embarked on a hiatus with a former employee who had rented a California seaside cabin. The couple traveled discreetly for three weeks until she was dropped off three miles from Agua Prieta where then she walked the remaining distance.

A Los Angeles Grand Jury intended to hold her legally accountable for the credibility of her story. A jury trial was scheduled for mid-January 1927, but never convened due to credibility issues with the case. The charges were dropped but Sister Aimee's integrity afterwards came under closer scrutiny and suffered from adverse publicity.

A passionate orator, Sister Aimee was linked later with numerous illicit romantic affairs. None were ever substantiated. Her elevated exposure made her the target of gossip and threats to reveal past indiscretions. By 1931, she added a security chaperone to guard against such frivolous allegations.

With the approach of the Great Depression, the popularity of her ministry waned along with an increase in organizational debt. She married again in September 1931 to actor and musician David Hutton. Their union was tainted from the outset.

Hutton rapidly imposed his surname into Semple-McPherson's charity work and touted himself as *Aimee's man*. During one of her spirited orations, she fainted and fractured her skull. While she recovered from her injury in Europe, he toured his cabaret singing act domestically embellishing his newfound celebrity with indiscreet photographs next to scantily clad women. His gleefully reported scandals in the press tainted the church's reputation. The couple separated in 1933 and divorced the year afterwards. She publicly repented of the marriage as *wrong from the beginning*. The taint caused her to decline a subsequent marriage proposal from a nationally known gospel singer in 1935.

No longer portrayed as a media darling or described as the *miracle woman* by the press, Semple-McPherson continued her ministry, but the tone of reporting had altered. Rumored scandals, accounts of internal organizational disputes and financial difficulties dominated their coverage of her. Sister Aimee modified her public persona by shedding weight, trimming and dying her hair and dressing stylishly. She appeared in frequent photo opportunities with celebrities and exploited theatrics more than ever in her sermons.

She became estranged from her mother and Rheba Crawford Splivato, one of her closest evangelistic peers. She cultivated a formidable adversary in evangelist Reverend Robert P. Shuler. Over the years following her death, his view of her personality and ministry softened until ultimately he acknowledged her contributions to the evangelical faith. Throughout even the darkest periods, she continued her ministry with fervor and maintained a loyal base of supporters.

On September 26, 1944, Sister Aimee traveled to Oakland to conduct a series of revivals preaching one of her popular sermon series *The Story of My Life*. The next morning, her son discovered her unconscious with pills and a half-empty bottle of capsules nearby. She was pronounced dead at

11:15 a.m. Amidst a lifetime littered with irony, her death became one of the most perplexing. Earlier that morning, she had called her personal physician to complain about feeling ill from her ingested medication. He was in surgery and could not respond to her call. She phoned another doctor, who referred her to a colleague. She lost consciousness before he could be contacted.

Her autopsy did not conclusively determine her cause of death. Among the pills discovered in her room were the sedative Seconal, which had not been prescribed for her. Despite speculation of suicide, her cause was reported as *Unknown*. The most consistently accepted explanation was that she died of an accidental overdose compounded by pre-existing kidney failure.

Forty-five thousand people waited in extended lines over three days to view her corpse lying in state at the Temple. An estimated eleven trucks transported memorial flowers to the cemetery with mourners crossing social class and color lines.

Despite her luminescence and former influence, the legacy of pioneer Aimee Semple McPherson is rarely recalled today. Her church remains operating, but her influential shadow became impossible to replace. Television evangelists today proliferate Sunday mornings and late night viewing slots. Sexual and financial scandals periodically resurface reminding caustic observers that television preaching resembles show business. Offerings and tithing money streams sustain the performances.

Whether God finds amusement or piety in these spectacles remains subject to personal perspectives regarding divine existence. Despite their spiritual quest for relevancy, each orator remains distinctly human and for all of the charity and positive works accomplished by their organizations, the question will continually hover as to the true motives and objectives behind their spiritual solicitations.

Angelus Temple
1100 Glendale Blvd, Los Angles

PHOTOS: Angelus Temple

Ned Doheny and Hugh Plunkett: The Greystone Mansion Killings

Greystone is a Tudor Revival style structure located within 18-acres of splendor in Beverly Hills. Architect Gordon Kaufmann designed the palatial estate in 1928. In a moneyed community obsessed by competing architecture, Greystone reigns distinct with its spacious elegance.

The main residence resembles an ostentatious English manor influenced by American tastes. The 55-room mansion includes a bowling alley with hidden bar, walls made of leaded glass, a main hall of checkered Carrara marble, a personal switchboard, secret passageways and grand rooms filled with European antiques. The grounds included an automated 80-foot waterfall, stables, riding trails, a swimming pool, kennel and Renaissance inspired Cypress Lane designed by landscape architect Paul Thiene.

The building is an ideal setting for mystery and intrigue. The estate has been often utilized in filming productions and is publicly accessible. Few visitors realize the tragic double homicide involving the original owner and his personal secretary.

The mansion was originally a gift bestowed by West Coast oil tycoon Edward Doheny to his son, Edward Ned Doheny, Jr. and his family.

The gift came amidst the chaos and political skirmishes involved with the national *Teapot Dome Scandal*. The scandal involved oil leases in Teapot Dome, Wyoming that were awarded to favored associates of Secretary of the Interior Albert Fall without competitive bidding. The fallout tarnished the presidency of Warren Harding and exposed an unprecedented level of corruption between one of his Cabinet members and moneyed oil interests. Both Dohenys and Ned's personal assistant Hugh Plunkett were questioned regarding their participation.

Edward faced indictment regarding a documented loan he had given to Fall, a former business associate. Ned and Hugh Plunkett had physically delivered the financial documents as functionaries.

The relationship between Doheny and his secretary Plunkett was unusual. They were considered close friends despite their class differences.

Ned lived a comfortable and affluent existence with all of the privileges of his aristocratic status. Plunkett originally worked at gas station owned by Ned's father-in-law and was later hired as a chauffeur for the Doheny family. Both men served in World War I. Upon their return, Plunkett became Ned's personal secretary, traveling as part of the family entourage.

Hugh married and lived modestly. Ned and his wife Lucy lived in extravagant excess bankrolled by his father's millions.

The consequences of legal entanglement for Plunkett could have been ruinous. His fate was left entirely in the hands of the Doheny legal team, whose priorities were clearly with their employer. During 1929, he and Ned were scheduled to be called in to testify on bribery charges concerning the loan. Their social division became evident when Ned was promised immunity from prosecution and Plunkett was not.

While Ned remained with his father and the legal team in Washington D.C., Plunkett oversaw the construction details involved with the family residence. Ned, his wife and their five children moved in during the final months of 1928. At the family's first Christmas celebration, the combined stress of the impending hearing and fatigue from the construction project stimulated a nervous breakdown by Plunkett.

By mid-February, family members noticed that his normal placid personality was unraveling. He refused their offer of a rejuvenate stay at a sanitarium. Plunkett's eleven-year marriage was dissolving. He couldn't sleep and was developing an unhealthy dependence on sleeping pills.

On the evening of February 16, 1929, Ned Doheny and Hugh Plunkett were shot to death by single bullets to each head. Tracing a plausible motive became as elusive as determining who fired the responsible weapon.

The Los Angeles police forensic director later published a book disputing the media accepted version that Plunkett had shot Doheny and then turned the gun on himself. Newspapers created a scenario where Ned had died attempting to help a troubled friend suffering from nervous exhaustion.

The controversially published evidence offered numerous conflicting facts. Investigator had found a smoldering cigarette in Hugh's lifeless fingertips, extraordinary for someone committing suicide. The gun used in the murder lay conveniently under Plunkett's body. The weapon was hot as though it had been heated in an oven.

The family doctor, under hostile investigative questioning, testified that Ned was still alive and breathing when he initially burst into the room. However, he was already slipping into unconsciousness and delirium.

Ned Doheny appeared to have been shot at very close

range. Plunkett was not. The forensic expert conjectured that the actual sequence and responsible party had been reversed from the publicly delivered account.

Still another theory suggested that Ned's wife Lucy had caught the two men together in a compromised position and shot both fatally. Rumors of a sexual liaison circulated following the killings based on the their close relationship but have never been substantiated.

Before the era of mass media exposure, wealthy family indiscretions remained hushed. The details behind Doheny and Plunkett's deaths evaded public scrutiny. The Los Angeles District attorney promised publicly a sweeping investigation. During this period, justice and disclosure within Los Angeles was for sale due to the unsavory influence of the *City Hall Gang*.

Edward Doheny had both the resources and contacts to effectively silence the investigation. The district attorney abruptly closed the inquiry before arriving at a conclusive resolution.

Both men were cremated and buried 100 feet apart at Forest Lawn Cemetery. Ned's ashes were interned in the magnificent temple of Santa Sabina, which once housed the bones of a second century Italian saint. Plunkett's were buried underneath the sod on Sunrise Slope. Hundreds attended Doheny's funeral while Plunkett's ceremony was modestly attended the following day. Lucy Doheny sent a huge floral arrangement to Plunkett's funeral and two of her brothers served as pallbearers. Scandal, animosity and disclosure were sealed permanently.

Lucy remarried and remained at Greystone until 1955. She sold the mansion and estate to Chicago based development interests. The new owners attempted to subdivide the property and demolish the mansion. The Beverly Hills city council prevented their plan. The city purchased the property in 1965 and ultimately converted it into its current public and private uses.

Both Doheny's and Plunkett were ultimately cleared of any criminal intent involved in their dealings with Albert Fall. The Interior Secretary's legacy concluded less favorably. He was convicted of conspiracy and bribery charges for accepting the loan, stripped of his Cabinet post and jailed for a year. In retribution for his greed and the ensuing complications, Doheny's corporation foreclosed on Fall's New Mexico home due to unpaid loans.

The owed sum turned out to be the identical amount that originally launched the *Teapot Dome Scandal* inquiry.

Greystone Mansion:
905 Loma Vista Drive, Beverly Hills

PHOTO: Greystone Mansion

Lee Francis: The Original Hollywood Madame

The allure of Hollywood and becoming a famous film actress has served as a magnet for young women since the industry's inception. The majority of transplants then as today never succeed. During the 1930s, the options for failure were twofold: either return home or remain participants in the sexual underground.

Lee Francis understood this dilemma and exploited the plentiful availability of young, attractive and financially desperate women. Migrating to Los Angeles from San Francisco in the 1920s, she established her base of prostitution operations in several rooms of the Hacienda Arms apartment complex in West Hollywood. Constructed in 1927, the Hacienda was designed in Italian Renaissance style architecture. The property was originally home to numerous motion picture actors including Marie Dressler, Loretta Young, James Dunn and Jeanette MacDonald.

During the 1930s, the building became better known as the *House of Francis* and was regarded as the most infamous West Coast brothel. The clientele was strictly upscale and reportedly featured such regulars as Clark Gable, Errol Flynn, Spencer Tracy, John Gilbert and a high-profile inventory of studio executives and distinguished personalities. One of her most unusual clients was actress Jean Harlow who paid Francis $500 to take customers home and accommodate her *rough sexual appetite*.

Francis kept her *open secret* operation scandal free by allegedly distributing 40% of her profits to police, lawyers and well-situated politicians. Periodic police raids generated no arrests as vice squad members were greeted with Russian caviar, French champagne and American cash. Motion picture studio *fixers* kept their stars away from media scrutiny and headlines with generous infusions of money to the press for non-reporting.

The system generally functioned smoothly until 1940 when Francis decided to limit and even cease her payoffs. Retribution was swift. The same year, her establishment was raided by a Los Angeles County sheriff's vice squad resulting in her and two employee's arrests. Her prison term was a mere 30 days, but the notoriety effectively ended her reign.

The building became known as the Coronet Apartments and was sold the following year. Changes in ownership and an absence of repairs and renovations prompted a steep decline in stature over the next three decades. Transients and counter culture groups inhabited the building during the late 1960s, but were cleared out during an intended 1970s renovation project.

Singer Rod Stewart and a business partner purchased the structure in the late 1970s with visions of converting the vacant building into a European-style luxury hotel. The concept never got off the ground as Stewart and his partner engaged in a bitter legal tussle over control. In 1982, Stewart was robbed at gunpoint as he was leaving the building in broad daylight. One year later, the building was nearly destroyed by a suspected arson fire.

The structure has subsequently been renovated and converted into luxury commercial office space and renamed the *Piazza del Sol*. A celebrity upscale Japanese restaurant fronts the building populated with distinguished diners and pretenders clothed in disaffected black outfits.

Hacienda Arms Apartment (Currently Piazza de Sol)
8439 Sunset Blvd, West Hollywood

PHOTOS: Piazza del Sol

The San Fernando Valley's Tree Lined Development Oasis

King Arthur's mythical kingdom of *Avalon* was briefly reincarnated amidst the San Fernando Valley pasturelands during the 1920s. The visionary land development of *Girard* was promoted as an exotic Turkish city complete with domes, minarets and fountains. At the centerpiece was a mosque-like structure located at the intersection of contemporary Ventura Boulevard and Topanga Canyon Boulevard.

Victor Girard Kleinberger dreamed up this improbable vision after his initial real estate speculation forced him into bankruptcy in 1921. Girard prudently dropped his Germanic last name, as it was post World War I. He acquired nearly 2,900 acres in the southwestern Valley region. Modestly he named the venture after himself, planted over 100,000 trees to beautify the region and positioned false fronts on existing shacks to create an impression of an expanding and thriving community.

He divided his acreage into 6,000 diminutive lots scarcely able to accommodate a small cabin. Armed with an aggressive sales force, the project sold and resold multiple land plots, frequently in identical locations. A touring bus was even commissioned to transport potential investors throughout the Los Angeles basin and the Cahuenga Pass before arriving at the mythical gates of Girard. At the peak of his marketing scheme in the mid 1920s, the development featured a school, newspaper, fire department and nursery, where even more trees were cultivated.

The ruse was destined to fail once Girard's duplicity was discovered. In 1929, a combination of massive homeowner lawsuits and the New York Stock Exchange crash hasten the end of his swindle. Within two years, most of the investor's and Girard himself had abandoned the sinking vessel. A few families remained through the Depression years.

The abundance of trees eventually proved useful for the land's subsequent reinvention. In 1941, the territory became a new community and named itself *Woodland Hills*.

Original Girard Corporate Headquarters
Corner Ventura Boulevard and Topanga Canyon Boulevard, Woodland Hills

The Love Market Escort Service

In the Spring of 1931, Southern California was treated to two sensational trials involving wealthy businessmen and a prostitution escort service labeled the *The Love Market*. What distinguished this operation from similar services was the *escorts* were reputedly under the legal age of consent.

Aspiring *actress* Olive Clark Day and movie publicist William Jobelmann reportedly supplied young and *inexperienced* girls as companions to wealthy men for weekend trips and parties. Their eagerly media reported *Girl Bazaar* auctioned high school aged girls to the highest male bidders. The *Love Market* stigma generated national attention, particularly when three of Day's supposed clients were outed publicly. The three included millionaires, John Mills, Jesse Shreve and famed theatre promoter Alexander Pantages.

Two trials staged in Los Angeles and San Diego exonerated everyone except Day, who was convicted and served marginal jail time. The sordid and poorly orchestrated trials effectively blackened the reputations of everyone involved.

The high school girls of *tender years* often proved less naive, innocent and young as reported. Day's operation involved mobility since she lacked the police protection shared by her more established competitors. She operated out of a Los Angeles residential address, often cited by her employees as *their* temporary living quarters.

Most of her logistical tryst arrangements involved hotels and were conducted by phone. Her biggest selling point remained offering clients *virgins* or *inexperienced girls*. The *girls* working for Day by her account came from a variety of backgrounds. Jobelmann recruited the majority from office buildings, secretarial schools, art classes, employment agencies and cruising expeditions on main streets. Jobelmann's experience in the motion picture industry assisted in recruiting *talent* from the thousands of aspiring but unsuccessful actresses drifting through Los Angeles.

For the sex workers, the profits from the liaisons were marginal compared to the organizers. Earned for the reported San Diego party staged at the El Cortez Hotel, Olive Clark Day was reportedly paid $200 per person for the services of each girl. In comparison, employee 17-year-old Camilla Clark confessed that she was driven by Day twice to a luxurious house on Point Loma Road where a man introduced to her as *Bill Martin* attacked her. For her efforts, Clark was given a $2 hat and a cheap coat.

As the sensationalism of the *Love Market* furor ebbed, public fascination evaporated. The majority of involved individuals returned to anonymity. Los Angeles District Attorney Buron Fitts who aggressively pursued and prosecuted the *Love Market* case seeking his own advancement would ultimately commit suicide. Accused promoter Alexander Pantages would die in his sleep in 1936 planning a fresh comeback based on Vaudeville theatres. During his storied life, he had owned eighty theatres at the height of his prosperity. He had liquidated all but the Hollywood Pantages before the stock market crash of 1929 demonstrating financial shrewdness or sound insider information.

Olive Clark Day's Operational Address
2573 Glen Green, Los Angeles

PHOTO: Olive Clark Day's Residence

Charles Crawford: The Fixer Loses His Influence

The *Tammany Hall* political machine dominated New York City politics between the mid 19th and 20th centuries. The Los Angeles equivalent of Charles Crawford and his *City Hall Gang* manipulated Los Angeles politics during the decade of the roaring 1920s.

The unelected kingmaker of Los Angeles, Crawford began his career operating dance halls and saloons in Seattle at the turn of the 20th century. He relocated and seamlessly integrated into southern California operating multiple casinos and bordellos. His activities cultivated influential political and law enforcement connections.

His influence shifted from vice to political Machiavellian. He and his associates sponsored candidate George E. Cryer victorious win for mayor of Los Angeles in 1921. For the next two terms while the city enjoyed unprecedented growth, Crawford became the primary fixer and influence peddler. His reputation and flamboyance were legendary during an era when excess was celebrated.

All roads towards city development, procurement favors and legal protection necessitated Crawford's cooperation and approval. His traditional sources of illicit revenue flowed directly into city government and dishonesty became institutionalized. His notorious greed and viciousness elevated public corruption into a new and elevated stench within Los Angeles.

Then the unforeseeable transpired.

In 1929, Cryer opted not to run for re-election and a reform candidate succeeded him. Abruptly out of power and losing his intimidating influence, a tide of media examination and

74

judicial scrutiny began focusing attention on Crawford and his activities. His power base was evaporating, He was indicted on bribery charges involving a city councilman and later a securities scandal. The charges for both counts were ultimately dismissed when reluctant witnesses refused to testify.

With the New York Stock market collapse and the effects of the Great Depression beginning, the grazing pastures for political dinosaurs were thinning.

Crawford sought professional legitimacy and sanctuary by opening an insurance and real estate office on the 6500 block of Sunset Boulevard in Hollywood. He publicly embraced the protestant faith and made very pretentious contributions to St. Paul's Presbyterian Church.

With his influence receding, his personal vulnerability was exposed to vicious published and finally physical attack. In May of 1931, Crawford and an associate Herbert Spencer were shot at close range during a private meeting with an unknown assailant in his office. Spencer was killed instantly. Crawford regained consciousness before undergoing emergency surgery. Consistent with his criminal code of silence, he refused to identify his shooter. The fatal bullet had ruptured his liver and one of his kidneys. He died on the operating table. His funeral procession was overflowing. Some of the attendees mourned while others wanted to certify he was indeed gone.

His clandestine operations soon became publicly disclosed and the veil of secrecy that he'd constructed, disintegrated. Several weeks following the shooting, David H. Clark, a prosecutor and judicial candidate emerged from the shadows to confess his guilt for the double homicide. A jury acquitted him twice of the crime based on a presumption of self-defense. A cigar, not a gun however was lifted from Crawford's dead hand.

After Clark was acquitted at his second retrial, the untidy inconvenience of Charles Crawford was laid to eternal rest. Clark would murder again in 1953 and die shortly after his imprisonment.

In 1936, Crawford's widow, Ella leveled his former offices and commissioned architect Robert V. Derrah to design an international outdoor shopping mall and office complex called the Crossroads of the World.

The kitsch stucco fantasy was self-promoted as America's first outdoor mall. The principal building resembles an ocean liner surrounded by a small village of cottage-style bungalows. Ella Crawford's intention presumably was to commemorate her husband's contribution to progress within Los Angeles. Instead she erected a testament of shame now weathering poorly and as archaic as influence peddling and derailed political machines.

The *Crossroads of the World* complex today hosts numerous entertainment industry production and publishing company offices. Like Charles Crawford, it symbolizes an individual that Los Angeles historians would prefer to forget. It is safe to conclude that most people already have.

Charles Crawford Murder:
6655 Sunset Boulevard, Hollywood

PHOTO:
Crossroads of the World commercial complex

Actress Peg Entwistle's Desperate Leap to an Unanticipated Fame

Hollywood evolved into the recognized symbol of the motion picture industry during the twentieth century. The film industry, however traces its legitimate roots to the terrain and urban environment of downtown Los Angeles. Many of the industry's initial founders were concentrated within the lodgings of Spring Street.

The genesis of commercial filmmaking is generally attributed to Thomas Edison's *Kinetoscope* viewing machine, which enabled viewers to peep into a magnified eyeglass viewers and observe the rapid rotation of photographed stilled images. His initial patent was recorded in 1890 and three years later, he assembled the first motion picture studio, the *Black Maria* in New Jersey.

His success bred imitation and the primitive technology continued to evolve into more sophisticated equipment, productions, viewing locations and ambitiously filmed storylines. The motion picture industry migrated west frequently to escape Edison's patent rights and legal pursuit. The still barely inhabited and diverse topography of the Los Angeles basin accommodated all forms of filming scenery, from the bustling urban downtown center to barren valleys. Los Angeles was a filmmaker's dream, absent of regulations, unions and permits. Creativity usually thrives with an absence of controls.

The silent film era flourished as traditional dramatic stage theatre's influence waned. Little has changed with regard to preference. Audiences still prefer entertainment novelty and technological advancements.

The migration of acting talent established its cradle within the lobby and confines of Spring Street's Alexandria Hotel. Nearly every major film personality and studio pioneer inaugurated his or her Los Angeles experience from the Alexandria. Among these major film players included Paramount, Griffith, Pathe, Chaplin, Leammle/Universal, Sennett/Keystone, Metro Goldwyn Mayer, United Artists and Warner Brothers. The list of permanent residents was even more impressive.

Many of these patriarchs of the film industry in the early days resided and dined together communally. The future architects of cinema shared the propelling forces of ambition in common. In 1900, a national vaudeville strike forced live theatres to project films. The films were crude, short but significantly less expensive than live talent. Many of the theatres permanently abandoned vaudeville performances and a proverbial technology star was birthed.

The Relocation of the Film Colony
The influence of the film colony within downtown Los Angeles history was abbreviated. The downtown film interests would eventually gravitate towards less expensive real estate in a development called *Hollywoodland*, then a population of 4,000 in 1910, adjacent to the Cahuenga Pass.

Hollywoodland initially was conceived and promoted from the 34 North Spring Street offices of Harvey Henderson Wilcox. Wilcox subdivided and conquered. In 1924, the iconic Hollywoodland sign was constructed at a cost of $21,000 atop Mount Lee. Thirteen 50-foot letters and four thousand 20-watt light bulbs announced change. The film industry would never return to downtown Los Angeles.

Peg Entwistle's Failed Ambitions
Millicent Lillian *Peg* Entwistle was a British stage and screen actress who had begun her career in 1925 at the age

of seventeen appearing in several Broadway productions. Her parents divorced when Peg was young and her father gained sole custody. She emigrated with him, her brothers and uncle from Liverpool to New York City aboard the SS Philadelphia at the age of five. At fourteen, a hit-and-run motorist on Park Avenue and 72nd Street in New York City tragically killed her father. Her uncle took in Peg. He was the manager of Broadway actor Walter Hampden.

For seven years her career on Broadway expanded and reviews for her roles, often comedic and good-hearted beauties were favorable. In 1927, she married actor Robert Keith. Their union was brief. Two years later she filed for divorce charging Keith with cruelty and failing to inform her that he'd been married before and had a six-year-old son. That son, Brian, would later become a celebrated actor and terminate his own life by suicide.

In 1932, the abrupt cancellation of the production *Alice Sit-by-the-Fire* became Entwistle's final Broadway performance. She moved to Los Angeles and secured her first theatre role in May with *The Mad Hopes* at the downtown Belasco Theatre. She was also cast in a small role in the Radio Pictures film *Thirteen Women* starring Myrna Loy and Irene Dunne. Her part portrayed her as a lesbian, too daring for the era. Upon its release in October, the viewing public and critics poorly received the film. *Thirteen Women* would be re-released in 1935 with further editing and cited favorably as one of the earliest female ensemble films.

As a probable cost cutting measure, Entwistle along with a contingent of other actresses did not have their contracts renewed by Radio Pictures (later RKO). The film would remain her sole cinematic credit and would be released the month following her tragic death.

On September 18, 1932, a woman hiking along the Hollywoodland sign discovered a female shoe, purse, and jacket. Inside the purse she discovered a suicide note. Scanning the horizon, she viewed the silhouette of a corpse. The woman reported her findings to the Los Angeles police and laid the items on the steps of the Hollywood police station.

The suicide note read: *I am afraid, I am a coward. I am sorry for everything. If I had done this a long time ago, I would have saved a lot of pain. P.E.*

Investigators speculated that two days before after telling her uncle she was going for a walk to the drugstore with friends, she hiked to the southern slope of Mount Lee at the base of the sign. Then readily accessible, she climbed a workman's ladder to the top of the initial letter H and leaped to her death. The coroner listed the cause of death as *multiple fractures of the pelvis.*

Police from the ravine below the sign recovered her body. She initially remained unidentified. Her uncle, whom she'd been living with, read the newspaper account about the anonymous victim and connected the reported initials P. E. with his niece who'd gone mysteriously missing. He identified the remains.

The attention that had formally eluded her became magnified globally upon her reported death. Her symbolic suicide would be interpreted as the fate destined for a successive legion of failed actresses. Her body was cremated and her ashes were interned next to her father's in Glendale, Ohio.

The Hollywoodland housing development went bankrupt

during the 1930s. The sign ownership rights and maintenance were transferred to the city of Hollywood. In 1949, the infamous H on the sign unexpectedly collapsed. The cause was attributed to adverse weather conditions, but explanations such as Entwistle's visitation circulated. During the course of renovations, the letters LAND were removed from the signage.

Over subsequent decades, neglect, deterioration and vandalism became the sign's greatest enemy.

Beginning with fundraising efforts in the late 1970s' renovations began on the sign including reinforcing the structure, repainting the letters and creating security fencing and monitoring to protect against unauthorized access.

To date, no additional notable performers have shared a similar fate to Peg Entwistle's. What precisely prompted her to commit suicide? Her uncle cited *depression* and *intense mental anguish*. During that period, her former husband Robert Keith had remarried. She was known to be impulsive and moody, but no one seemed to anticipate her extreme action.

Sightings of a disoriented blonde woman have periodically resurfaced. The apparition is often conveniently accompanied by the smell of gardenias, her perfume of preference. Return haunting by the celebrated departed is never particularly surprising. With her novel iconic demise, the elusive fame Peg Entwistle sought while living was finally realized.

Peg Entwistle's Jumping Off Point:
Hollywood Sign
South Facing Slope Mount Lee, Hollywood Hills

PHOTOS: Hollywood Sign and close up of one of the letters circa 1982

(1982)

Ross Alexander: A Transitioning Actor Abruptly Lowers the Stage Curtain

Ross Alexander began his acting career on the stage appearing in production in Boston and Broadway. He was regarded as a promising leading actor due to his charm, good lucks and approachable style.

In the early 1930's, Paramount Pictures signed him to a film contract. His initial 1932 debut in *The Wiser Sex* fared poorly at the box office. Two years later, he briefly returned to Broadway to resume his stage career. The relocation was short-lived as in 1934 he signed another film contract with Warner Brothers. He was typecast as a polished and well-dressed leading man. Two of his films *A Midsummer Night's Dream* and *Captain Blood* in 1935 achieved modest success.

In February 1934, Alexander married actress Aleta Freel in New Jersey. The union was brief and troubled. Freel shot herself to death in December 1935. Shortly over nine months later, he married Anne Nagel, whom he had appeared with in two films.

Alexander's life was chaotic and plagued by debt and depression. Only three months following his second marriage, he shot himself fatally in the barn behind his home. His final film *Ready, Willing and Able* was released posthumously. His former home and barn are currently boutique stores along retail saturated Ventura Boulevard. Aleta Freels' home is nestled high in Hollywood hills as difficult to access as both of their careers are to remember.

Aleta Freel Suicide Location
7357 Woodrow Wilson Drive, Hollywood

Ross Alexander Residence
17221 Ventura Boulevard, Encino

PHOTOS: Aleta Freel's former residence and site of Ross Alexander's former house and barn.

Ted Healy: The Suspected Homicide of the Fourth Stooge

Ted Healy is credited as being the creator of the Three Stooges act and a style of slapstick comedy that has increasingly lessened in popularity due to its overt sexism and violent tendencies.

Healy was originally a successful vaudeville performer and considered the highest paid performer during the 1920s. The original concept behind his creation of the Stooges was to invite planted cast members (stooges) and hecklers from an audience during a serious acrobat routine and encourage improvisational mayhem.

Audiences adored the unforeseen results and his show became wildly successful.

Moses Horwitz (known as Moe Howard) was Healy's childhood friend and initial recruit. Moe's brother Shemp joined the act in 1923 and Larry Fine was added in 1928.

The chemistry onstage disintegrated backstage. Cast members quit, returned and the group frequently quarreled and reorganized. In 1929, the quartet appeared in several Broadway productions. Wider exposure came with their appearance in the 1930 film Soup to Nuts.

The success of their subsequent films ultimately diminished Healy's control. The Howard brothers and Fine separated from Healy's troupe over contract disputes. The trio began performing apart and established their own professional identity. Healy sued them for using his gimmickry and routines. The Shubert Theatre Company owned the copyrights to the show and produced the trio's work. Healy was frozen out of the proceeds,

He attempted to replicate his own competitive version of the Stooges and the other original members frequently collaborated with him despite their legal dispute. Curly Howard replaced his brother Shemp and by 1934, the Howard brothers had professionally parted ways with Healy entirely. Healy appeared in a succession of films integrating new Stooges into the cast.

His personal life was as chaotic as his on stage character. He twice married impulsively, divorced, reconciled and later fathered a son John Jacob with his second estranged wife. Ted would die four days before his birth celebrating at the famed Hollywood Trocadero nightclub. He was 41-years-old.

The circumstances behind his demise on that December 20, 1937 evening have never officially been verified. He was initially presumed to be the victim of a heart attack. The controversy surrounding preceding events prompted the treating physician's refusal to sign his death certificate.

At the Sunset Strip club, a heated argument escalated between Healy and three reported college- aged boys. There have been subsequent but unconfirmed suggestions that the boys were actually actor Wallace Berry and two film producers. The younger men knocked Healy to the ground and proceeded to kick him in the head, ribs and abdomen. He was clearly injured, bloodied, and incoherent after the beating and returned by taxi to his apartment.

He expired the next morning. Autopsy findings revealed that Healy died of acute toxic nephritis and chronic alcoholism. The external wounds from the fight were specifically ruled out as his direct cause of death.

Not everyone was convinced by the findings. No one however was ever arrested.

Despite his earnings, Healy flagrantly overspent and died destitute. His friends and colleagues established a trust fund to financially support his widow and son.

His son would later change his name to Theodore John Healy in honor of his late father. He lived a more conventional lifestyle in the Atlanta area. He joined the U.S. Naval Academy, served a tour of duty in Vietnam, married, became a schoolteacher and later a financial planner. He passed away in 2011

Today the Hollywood Trocadero nightclub site is integrated into a sequence of shops and restaurants. The Hollywood of yesteryears has vanished. The Three Stooges are unknown to most individuals under the age of forty. Their infrequent telecasts are consigned to extreme late night television viewing.

Ted Healy is rarely mentioned in the same conversation as the Howard Brothers. Hardcore fans and archivists exclusively remember his contribution. Many viewers today with society's modified social consciousness question why people ever considered violent slapstick to be funny in the first place.

Ted Healy Homicide:
Former Trocadero Club location, corner of Sunset Boulevard and Sunset Plaza Drive, Hollywood

PHOTO:
Location of the original Trocadero Club

The Sleepy Lagoon Murder and Zoot Suit Riots

It seems inconceivable today that a fashion style could incite nationwide riots emulating that, which occurred most notably in Los Angeles between June 3-8, 1943. The provocation and violence was racially motivated, but the culprit stimulated by an obscure Latino murder and wardrobe flaunting an excess of fabric.

On August 2, 1942, Jose Gallardo Diaz was discovered unconscious and dying along the 5500 block of Slauson Avenue in Commerce. This stretch of road was near a swimming reservoir called *Sleepy Lagoon*. Diaz never regained consciousness and his autopsy revealed that he had been inebriated from the evening before and had suffered a fracture at the base of his skull.

The fracture may have been induced by an automobile accident, repeated falls in his drunken state or activities resulting from a party he had attended the previous night. The Los Angeles Police Department promptly interrogated 600 Latino youths and arrested 17 suspects presuming Diaz's death was the result of a rival gang brawl. Despite little tangible evidence and inadequate defense representation, twelve of the defendants were convicted of second-degree murder on January 13, 1943. They were sentenced to San Quentin Prison. Conspicuously during the trial, the defendants were not allowed to communicate with their legal representatives nor permitted to change their clothing that consisted of contemporary stylish zoot suits.

The zoot suits struck a decisive nerve amongst many trial observers and a prejudicial presiding judge. The outfits necessitated extensive fabric perceived as *unpatriotic* due to World War II fabric rationing then imposed. The rationale employed by the judge and zealous American

91

nationalists was that the outfits were only worn by *hooligans* and represented an overt defiance towards the American war effort. These perceptions strongly influenced the jury's deliberations and ultimate verdict.

For wearers, the flamboyant styles created a distinct fashion statement representing a fresh wave of individualism, cultural distinctiveness, hairstyling and musical preference. Zoot suit material accentuated colorful fabric, extensive length (often reaching past the knees), exaggerated shoulder cuts and ruffled slacks. This protest against uniformed conformity extended into accessories that often accentuated chains and leather soled-shoes.

Nearly a year after Jose Diaz's death and months after the trial, the initial skirmishes between uniformed military personnel and Mexican-American Zoot Suitors began. What started as isolated scuffles escalated into widespread mob frenzy covered by national media. The East Los Angeles barrios became flashpoints for confrontation. The attacks escalated into additional ethnic neighborhoods and other cities nationally.

Sensing the excessive violence undermined the war effort, the Navy and Marine Corps ordered their command staffs to declare Los Angeles off-limits to all military personnel. Sailors and Marines were confined to their barracks. The riots subsided. In the midst of the frenzy, the Los Angeles City Council approved a resolution criminalizing the wearing of zoot suits within the city's limits.

In October 1944, California's Court of Appeals unanimously reversed the convictions of the twelve defendants in the Sleepy Lagoon murder. The court also criticized the judge for bias and his mishandling of the case. Relations between the Los Angeles police department and East Los Angeles barrios deteriorated irrevocably.

Today, the stretch of Slauson Avenue where Jose Diaz's body was discovered is a light industrial park. A prominent City of Commerce welcoming sign is located in the center island nearby.

The murder case and subsequent riots have been recreated in contemporary stage and cinema productions. Los Angeles would suffer racial flare-ups and subsequent riots in 1965 and 1992. The roots provoking cultural and racial unrest remain stubbornly entrenched. Prejudice, ignorance and vengeance are as elusive to eradicate as difficult to rationalize.

Sleepy Lagoon Murder Site:
5500 Slauson Avenue, City of Commerce

PHOTO: Sleepy Lagoon Murder Site

Lupe Velez: The Fatal Scruples of a Fiery Actress

Maria Guadalupe Villalobos was born in 1918 in the city of San Luis Potosi, Mexico and became Hollywood's first Latina star under the professional name Lupe Velez. One of five children, her prominent family sent her to study English and dance in San Antonio, Texas at the age of thirteen. During the early 1920's, Velez performed in the Mexican vaudeville circuit. Her suggestive singing and provocative dancing made her one of the most popular performers on the circuit.

In 1926, she was invited by telegram to perform as a cantina singer in a Los Angeles theatre production of *The Dove*. She arrived to discover that the part in the play had been given to another actress. While in Los Angeles, she met comedian Fanny Brice who recommended her to Flo Ziegfeld. He hired her to perform in New York City, but before she could depart, she was offered a screen test for a Metro-Goldwyn-Mayer film production. Producer and director Hall Roach saw the screen test and hired her for a small part in a Laurel and Hardy film *Sailors, Beware!*

Velez's career quickly ascended with parts in numerous film productions. She flawlessly made the transition from silent to talking films and carved a niche in comedy, playing beautiful but volatile characters. In 1932, she took a break from films and performed on Broadway as *Conchita* in the Ziegfeld musical *Hot-Cha!*

Throughout the 1930s, Velez's career endured plateaus and dips, but she finished the decade strongly with a series of eight films where she was typecast as the *Mexican Spitfire*, a temperamental yet congenial Mexican singer married to an elegant American gentleman. She parlayed this role along with other romantic comedy roles until 1944 when she returned to Mexico to play in an adaptation of Emile Zola's novel *Nana*. It would be her final film.

Velez became a living contradiction to her self-perception promoting a flamboyant public persona of lively exhibitionism and loud clothing. She attended Friday night boxing matches ringside at the Hollywood Legion Stadium. Gossip tabloids chronicled her tempestuous romantic relationships and jealous rages. Velez supplied many of the embellishments personally. She could be scathing and vicious towards rival actresses. By contrast she viewed herself in interviews as *simple and natural Lupe*.

She married actor Johnny Weissmuller in October 1933 and filed for divorce three times over the next six years charging him with *cruelty*. Their divorce was finalized in 1939. She reportedly had affairs with many of her leading actors and was linked to several highly publicized and stormy relationships. Several ended when the men refused to leave their wives.

In 1944, she began dating a struggling Austrian actor named Harold Ramond, eight years her junior. In September, she discovered she was pregnant. She announced publicly in late November that they were engaged. Ramond did not want the child and gave her the impression he would only marry her to *give the baby a name*. She kicked him out of her house.

This humiliation proved excessive for the impulsive Velez. On the evening of December 13, 1944, the 36-year old Velez dined with silent film star Estelle Taylor and Venita Oakie. The dinner conversation was probably unsettling with Velez vowing she would kill herself before consenting to an abortion to terminate her pregnancy. In the late evening hours, she retired to her bedroom and consumed 70

Seconal pills over a glass of brandy. Her secretary found her on her bed later that morning with a suicide note nearby. The text of the note asked God's forgiveness for her act and a condemnation of Ramond for his *faked love* towards her and the baby.

Ramond's film career ultimately went nowhere. Lupe Velez's death was parodied in Kenneth Anger's imaginative 1959 book *Hollywood Babylon* by recounting that her stomach rejected the lethal dose of barbiturates and she vomited in her bathroom toilet. There, she passed out and drowned in the water.

The toilet tale was likely fictional, but not entirely inconceivable for an actress diva that lived as flagrantly emotionally as she acted.

Lupe Velez Residence
732 North Rodeo Drive, Beverly Hills

PHOTO: Lupe Velez's House

Howard Hughes' Dangerous Navigating Habits

Among eccentric billionaire Howard Hughes' passions, the piloting of aircraft remained foremost. One of his prized acquisitions was a 100 XF-11 plane contracted by the US Army Air Material Command through his Hughes Aircraft company. The aircraft was reportedly then one of the world's fastest planes, attaining speeds in excess of over 400 miles per hour. Upon the conclusion of World War II, the need for the reconnaissance planes diminished making the project expendable. The military cancelled their contract for eleven aircraft, but allowed Hughes to complete two prototypes

On July 7, 1946, Hughes piloted one of planes on its maiden flight above the Los Angeles skies. He attempted to crash land the plane on the Los Angeles Country Club golf course but landed 300 feet short clipping treetops en route due to his low altitude.

The plane's right wing sliced through a two-story house at 803 N. Linden Drive and caromed off the garage at the rear of the residence. It then plowed into and settled atop the four-bedroom home of Lt. Colonel Charles Meyer, an interpreter at the war crime trials in Europe at 808 N. Whittier. The airplane burst into flames leaving only an assemblage of ruin. The house miraculously survived eventually requiring extensive remodeling to the roof and upper living quarters. One of the airplane's massive radial engines tore from its mount and was hurtled in excess of 60 feet tearing a huge gash into the adjacent house at 810 N. Whittier Drive.

Hughes was lifted from the wreckage severely injured, transported to Good Samaritan Hospital in Los Angeles and given even odds to survive. He lived but suffered third degree burns. On April 5, 1947, he would fly the second XF-11 prototype on its first test flight and seven months later, pilot his famed Spruce Goose on its only flight. Some observers claim this near-death experience initiated his perilous decent into bizarre behavior and reclusivenes. He died in April 1976 leaving more speculation about his life than answers.

New owners slated the Meyer house, constructed in 1926 by architect Wallace Neff for demolition in late 2013. The Beverly Hills Cultural Heritage Commission then intervened. In 2014, it was designated as a registered historical property. Perhaps only in Beverly Hills would a fiery collision and potential catastrophe merit historical perpetuity.

The airplane fiasco was not Hughes' first collision episode. On July 11, 1936, 30-year old Hughes fatally struck 59 year-old Gabe Meyer in a crosswalk at Third Street and Lorraine Boulevard. Hughes' speeding Duisenberg careening around the corner hitting Meyer, an employee at the May Company furniture department.

Hughes had arrived in Los Angeles a decade earlier with a $5,000 daily trust fund at his disposal. That fateful evening, he had been partying and after several witness came forward, he was charged with vehicular manslaughter. After the accident, Hughes was taken to the hospital and certified as *sober*. The attending doctor made a note that Hughes *had* been drinking.

By the time of the coroner's inquest, the key witness had changed his story to concur with Hughes passenger Nancy Bayly (Watts). Both claimed that Meyer moved directly in front of Hughes' car resulting in his accidental death. Hughes was held *blameless* by the coroner's jury and told reporters *I was driving slowly and a man stepped out of the darkness in front of me*.

The other eyewitnesses vanished and Hughes paid Meyer's relatives $10,000 *in their time of need*.

Howard Hughes Airplane Crash Site
808 N. Whittier, Beverly Hills

Hughes Fatal Collision with Gabe Meyer
484 South Lucerne Boulevard, Los Angeles

PHOTOS: Airplane crash site and fatal intersection

The Continued Fascination With the Black Dahlia Murder

What is it about the lurid murder and severed torso of 22-year-old Elizabeth Short that still fascinates? On the morning of January 15, 1947, Short's nude body was discovered in two pieces on an empty lot in the Leimert Park residential complex being constructed nearby the Los Angeles Memorial Coliseum. Today, the vacant space has been replaced by a nondescript single-level house and lawn, indistinguishable from others in the neighboring tract.

Elizabeth Short's brief life was similarly ordinary. The press sensationalized her biography as a call girl and adventuress. The mundane truth is that her life was far from sensational. She had shuffled residences between her bi-coastal divorced parents. She suffered from asthma and bronchitis. She lived and worked in various West Coast cities. She was once arrested at sixteen for underage drinking.

Her juvenile arrest remains our predominant visual image of Elizabeth Short. Her black and white mugshot features a stunning symmetrical face with pronounced cheekbones, curly raven hair and haunting penetrating eyes that rivet our attention. Frothing newspaper coverage erroneously nicknamed her the *Black Dahlia* while following her sensationalized murder. The reference came from a film noir murder mystery film released several months earlier called *The Blue Dahlia*.

Historically unsolved murders within California are not uncommon. Typically, more publicized and notorious killings prompt more creative suppositions. The search for Elizabeth Short's killer fueled paths to many suspects, purported confessions, speculations, books and film adaptations of the story. Each theory has lacked a provable ending and the fascination towards investigation continues unimpeded by the impossibility of resolution.

The shocking brutality and inhumanity of her murder eludes contemporary novelty based on a desensitized public. Modern television and film graphically depict similar visually abusive images. Digital technology has enabled us to view unimaginable horror from a detached perspective.

In 1947, despite following a cataclysmic global war with millions of innocent casualties, Americans remained susceptible to outrage and absorption about one single senseless homicide, The continued public fascination over Elizabeth Short's isolated death still defies explanation. Sadly, justice for her killing, even over seventy years after the fact becomes more imaginative than possible.

Black Dahlia Killing Site:
3825 South Norton Avenue, Los Angeles

The Mob Permanently Severs Relations With Bugsy Siegel

Post-World War II American gangster lore found its iconic hero in the guise of Benjamin *Bugsy* Siegel, The charismatic and outrageously perceived Siegel was the celebrated public face of organized crime making him a prominent target.

His reputation for violence and ruthlessness made him both feared and respected amongst friends, associates and rivals. Siegel's organization began with bootlegging during Prohibition and expanded later into more lucrative drug, protection, murder and prostitution operations. His greatest skill may have been his ability to forge alliances with diverse crime families effectively creating organized crime.

Beneath his cultivated public veneer as a flashy dresser, womanizer, and pseudo celebrity, Siegel was marginally more than a common hoodlum. He had compiled a criminal record that included armed robbery, rape and murder dating back to his teenage years. He detested the moniker *Bugsy* branded to him due to his sometimes ferocious intensity bordering on psychotic. He wished to be regarded as a sophisticate, but such reverence was personally unattainable.

His most insightful enterprise proved to be his promotion of gambling operations in the then near barren desert of Las Vegas. Seizing an opportunity to be perceived as a legitimate businessman in 1945, Siegel coerced William Wilkerson, by threat of death, to sell his entire stake of the under construction Flamingo Hotel to the mob. Siegel hired himself in the role of operations director.

His aim was to control the totality of Las Vegas' gambling

potential. The Flamingo would become his showpiece and headquarters. Siegel understood that a gambling destination would likewise require tourist amenities to tap into a secondary market of vacationers. In 1945 Las Vegas seemed as far removed from most tourism itineraries as the Sahara Desert.

History concurred with Siegel's vision, but he would not be allowed to witness its fulfillment. In 1946, the construction cost overruns for his signature palace had far exceeded initial estimates. Siegel's quest for extravagance and personal enrichment significantly surpassed his budget. His financial accountability proved vague. A habitual criminal rarely perceives financial discipline with the same stewardship as a traditional corporate CEO. Squandering other people's money is never a practice ensuring professional longevity.

Money was vanishing and the official opening date festivities of December 26, 1946 were a disaster. For the ceremony, the property and amenities remained unfinished and the normally stable weather rained a deluge. The catastrophe worsened as after two weeks, the gaming tables were operating at an inconceivable loss. By the conclusion of the first month, operations were shuttered.

Three months later, the casino was reopened and began cultivating positive press and profitability. Siegel was offered an opportunity for redemption, but the agreement proved a charade. Associates and superiors were simultaneously formulating plans to eliminate him from meetings in Havana.

Siegel's arrogance and boasting façade were affronts to an organization that insisted upon discretion and secrecy, especially since their activities were illegal.

On the evening of June 20, 1947, Siegel and an associate were lounging at his girlfriend Virginia Hill's Beverly Hills home. The residential property is easily accessible from the street and the landscaping makes concealment simple. The mobster, whose own national syndicate was nicknamed *Murder Incorporated*, became a victim by an assailant who fired at him through a viewing window with a .30 caliber military M1 carbine. Siegel was struck multiple times including two fatal head wounds.

The surprise and fury of the attack eliminated any opportunity for return response. The shadow of Bugsy Siegel was gone and his violent assassination proved instrumental in thrusting Las Vegas into national media exposure. He was only 41. Within days of his death, another crime family took over the operations of the Flamingo Hotel and Casino. Siegel's promotional legacy proved more valuable with the man himself absent.

Today he would likely revel with paternal pride at contemporary Las Vegas. The gambling and entertainment colossus ultimately matched and far exceeded his dream. Organized crime has presumably disappeared from a dominant influential and operational role. At least, that is the narrative promoted by the local Chamber of Commerce and a Gangster Museum honoring the dubious mob era.

Have they really left and why should they?

Criminality has the capacity to adorn the clothing of respectability as effortlessly as Siegel could be replaced. Perception is eternally subject to modification.

Bugsy Siegel Shooting Site:
810 North Linden Drive, Beverly Hills

PHOTO:
Mansion where the contract killing was committed

Carol Landis: The Insufficiency of Only Beauty

Carol Landis established her reputation as a competent actress and singer based on an aesthetically shaped hourglass profile. She was known as *The Ping Girl* and *The Chest* for her curvaceous figure and uninhibited flowing blond hair.

Her blond locks were dyed, her first name derived from her favorite actress Carol Lombard and her career trajectory followed a Hollywood screenplay. She was born in Wisconsin and at four moved with her family to San Bernardino. She dropped out of high school to pursue her show business dream. Her ascent couldn't have been more unlikely. She began as a cheesy hula dancer in a San Francisco nightclub and was rumored to have been hired out of pity. She later sang with a dance band until she had saved $100 and moved to Hollywood.

She appeared as an extra in the 1937 film *A Star is Born* and acted uncredited in various films labeled as *horse operas* since they typically featured a cowboy singing to his horse. She modeled for hundreds of provocatively fleshy posed photographs that were mass distributed.

Additional bit roles followed her path as a contract actress until she was launched into stardom with her portrayal as a cave girl in the film *One Million B.C.* Her positive reviews weren't based on her emotional vulnerability in delivering lines, but rather the fabric challenged outfits she was squeezed into.

During the early 1940s, she enjoyed a stream of successful motion pictures often cast as a second female lead. Her singing talent was considered good enough to be used in musicals. Part of her casting success was attributed to her relationship with Twentieth Century-Fox studio head Darryl F. Zanuck. When she ended their relationship, her career stalled and she was no longer offered premium film roles. During World War II, she toured with numerous USO troupes and became a popular pin-up poster with servicemen.

Landis' personal life mirrored the turbulence of her professional career. She was married four times and had no children. She was unable to conceive due to endometriosis. None of her marriages lasted long, but she had little difficulty attracting male overtures.

During her separation from fourth husband, Broadway producer W. Horace Schmidlapp, Landis began an affair with actor Rex Harrison who was married to actress Lili Palmer. Harrison refused to divorce his wife and Landis became despondent. On the evening of July 4, 1948, the pair shared dinner together. The next afternoon, Harrison and Landis' maid discovered her body at her home on the bathroom floor.

The 29-year-old Landis had taken a fatal overdose of Seconal. The scandal deepened when it was reported that she'd left two suicide notes, one for her mother and the other for Harrison. He would deny the affair publicly, reportedly instruct his lawyers to destroy the second suicide note and profess ignorance to the County Coroner as to a motive behind her suicide. He attended her funeral with his wife.

Carol Landis' Residence
1465 Capri Drive, Pacific Palisades

PHOTO: Carol Landis' Residence

Barbara Graham: An Unsympathetic Film Portrayal

Barbara Graham was a genuinely calloused and doomed figure while she lived. She earned the notorious distinction of becoming the third woman in California to be executed in the gas chamber in 1955. She became the inspiration for an Academy Award portrayal by actress Susan Hayward in the 1958 film *I Want to Live!* along with a later 1983 television remake.

The film portrayed Graham as an insensitive but questionably innocent victim caught up in a male orchestrated botched robbery that resulting in the violent death of Mabel Monohan. Monohan received no compassionate treatment by her perpetrators. She was mercilessly dispatched for being an uncooperative object of erroneous prison gossip.

There was little about Graham's biography or attributed quotes that suggested that she was innocent or merited compassion. Her life was a succession of poor choices and occasionally unintentional funny quotes.

She was born to an unmarried mother in 1925 and life's misfortunes accelerated from that inauspicious beginning. At two, her teenager mother was condemned to reform school. Graham followed her example throughout her teenage years eventually attending the identical institution after being arrested for vagrancy. She exhibited little inclination or ambition to complete her education and didn't.

She made a superficial attempt at reformation. In 1940, she married a US Coast Guardsman, had two children and enrolled in a business college. After three years, she abandoned her studies, marriage, and the constraints of a conventional life. She lost custody of her two sons, a nearly impossible outcome from that era.

Her failed lifestyle experiment resulted in a new and predictable occupation. She became a *seagull*, nicknamed for prostitutes flocking near naval bases. During World War II, she serviced a Pacific Corridor clientele including ports in Oakland, Alameda, Long Beach and San Diego. Her attractive appearance, flaming red hair and engaging personality made her desirable. She earned a distinction for working briefly in one of famed San Francisco Madame Sally Sanford's brothels. Sanford would augment her own legend by later becoming Mayor of Sausalito.

Graham's life of prostitution introduced her into associations with hardened criminals, gamblers and drug abusers. She mirrored their excesses. She spent portions of the next decade in jail and crowned her free fall by a marriage to bartender Henry Graham in 1953. With Graham, she had another son and found her *soulmate*, a hardened anti-social personality and drug addict.

Barbara embraced two friends of Graham, Jack Santo and Emmett Perkins. Consistently in character, she began an affair with Perkins, who confided with her about a story the pair had overheard in prison. The tale centered around Mabel Monohan, a 64-year-old widow who allegedly kept large amounts of cash hidden in her suburban Burbank home. The stash was stored on behalf of her gambling former son-in-law, Tutor Scherer.

In March 1953, Barbara Graham, Santo and Perkins teamed up with two associates, John True and Baxter Shorter (a professional safecracker). The loosely assembled gang schemed to loot Monohan's house one evening. Graham's role was to gain entry into the house by posing as a distressed victim experiencing car trouble. She innocently asked to use the widow's telephone. The ruse worked perfectly and enabled the other gang members to rush inside the house.

It was the singular aspect of their plan that succeeded.

The five demanded money and jewels from Monohan who stubbornly refused to divulge anything. She understood the desperate nature of criminality but underestimated their capacity for impulsive violence.

Graham (or another member) pistol-whipped Monohan for her obstinacy, cracking her skull. Her accomplices then suffocated the prostrate woman, silencing the sole source for locating the object of their break-in. The robbery attempt was futile as nothing of value was recovered despite a thorough ransacking of the house. What the team of imbeciles were rumored to have overlooked was nearly $15,000 in jewels and valuables concealed in a purse within a closet near the prone body of Monohan.

The murder and absence of motive seemed incoherent to investigating police. Desperate for suspects, five career criminals, including three former associates of gangster Mickey Cohen were arrested. Cohen's gambling operations had once been entrenched in the nearby Toluca Lake district and protected by the Burbank Police Department. In 1951, a California Crime Commission investigation into their comfortable arrangement resulted in the resignation of the police chief, mayor and a councilman.

One of the random five arrested was the safecracker Baxter Shorter. He was the sole individual actually present at the aborted robbery and murder. Shorter panicked over the prospects of facing the death penalty alone and immediately recounted a version of the events.

He embellished details to minimize his role. He confessed that he'd been used only as a lookout and had witnessed the pistol-whipping by Perkins and not Graham. He was horrified to have been associated with a murder. He elaborated that he had called the police department within hours following the tragedy in the hopes of saving the dying Monohan. A dispatcher error led a summoned ambulance to a nonexistent Los Angeles address instead of Burbank.

Shorter potentially may have avoided prosecution for the murder. His duplicity hadn't escaped the notice of his partners once police released him. He was promptly kidnapped by Perkins and Santo from his downtown Los Angeles apartment and relocated to a grave in the San Jacinto Mountains. His body was never recovered.

Lacking a principal witness, the prosecution for the murder stalled. Perkins and Santo were arrested for Shorter's kidnapping after being identified by his widow. Barbara Graham was equally occupied during the same span. She was arrested for passing over $250 worth of fraudulent checks.

Perkins and Santo were released due to the lack of body, but immediately detained by Burbank Police for Monohan's murder. By June 1953, a fragile case was being constructed against Perkins, Santo, Graham and True for Monohan's murder. The fabric was based principally on hearsay evidence by a periphery ex-con.

Fortunately for prosecutors, John True cracked under the strain of suspicion and agreed to turn state's evidence. With all of the potential defendants locked up, he opted to accept the identical terms Shorter was offered for his testimony.

Graham, who protested her innocence throughout, undermined her credibility by attempting to purchase an alibi from an ex-con associate. She was unaware that her potential alibi was working in conjunction with investigators. Their conversations were recorded. The press during the sensational trial labeled her *Bloody Babs* for lack of a more imaginative moniker.

John True's substantiated testimony and circumstantial evidence ultimately enabled a jury to convict Graham, Perkins and Santo of all the murder and robbery charges. True disappeared from public view following his controversial testimony.

Graham, Perkins and Santo were sentenced to death and their simultaneous executions were scheduled for June 3, 1955 at 10 p.m. Perkins and Santo were expediently dispatched without protest. Graham's execution was delayed for nearly two hours as her attorneys vainly petitioned California Governor Knight for clemency. The pause proved ideal for her screenplay martyrdom and notable quotations.

The negotiations prompted agonized outbursts from Graham beginning with her first. *Why do they torture me like this? I can't take this. Why didn't they let me go at ten? I was ready to go at ten.*

Once the governor conclusively denied her petition, she was led into the gas chamber. She begged for a blindfold and was given a sleep mask by an attending jail matron.

Her second public utterance evaded any semblance of remorse or request for forgiveness. Instead she condemned her accusers. Good people are always so sure they're right.

The irrepressible Graham capped her defiance when one of the men in charge of her execution offered her advice on making the passing easier and quicker for her by inhaling deeply. She responded, *How the hell would you know?*

The insolent murderer had miraculously assembled a literate body of proponents during her trial and following her execution. Their wrath over injustice apparently found the realities accompanying her life inconvenient additions to their indignation. Critics of capital punishment rallied behind her cause, employing the manipulative vehicles of motion pictures and books to eulogize her as a dupe of male victimizers and media sensationalism.

The question more appropriately asked should be ultimately who duped who?

Mabel Monohan Murder:
1718 West Parkside Avenue, Burbank

Johnny Stompanato: A Fatal Attraction

Johnny Stompanato was born in the Midwest into an immigrant middle-class family, the youngest of four children. His mother died six days after giving birth and his father soon remarried.

He attended the Kemper Military School in Boonville, Missouri and following graduation, like most of his generation, joined the military in the midst of World War II. He became a Marine and served in the Asian and the South Pacific theatre. He was discharged from the Corps in March 1946.

Like many returning veterans, his homecoming into civilian life proved complicated. For Stompanato, discerning good from evil entanglements was no longer simply a matter of fighting a hostile enemy. Relocating to Los Angeles, he opened and managed a gift shop selling inexpensive crude pottery and woodcarvings. The enterprise became a front for his primary activities as a bodyguard and enforcer for gangster Mickey Cohen. Cohen's enterprises controlled the majority of Los Angeles' vice activities.

The emergence of organized crime expanded into major metropolitan cities post-war. A surplus of unemployed and trained war killers was available for mob employment.

Stompanato was known for his handsome appearance, rashness and bodybuilding physique. In 1956, he began a romantic adventure with actress Lana Turner. Turner had reached a critical decline in her career. She had recently turned forty, appeared in a succession of box office flops and lost the financial security of her contract with MGM Pictures. Her liaison with Stompanato would prove toxic for both parties.

Their relationship was consistently stormy, punctuated by arguments, aggression, and his frequent beatings.

Turner took advantage of an acting opportunity by appearing in an English film *Another Time, Another Place*, co-starring an emerging young actor Sean Connery. Connery successfully seduced Turner during the filming and the international press explicitly reported their sightings together and flowering relationship.

Stompanato became livid with jealousy and impulsively flew over to England. With customary impatience, he stormed the film set and threatened Connery with a gun. Connery, who would cement his future acting reputation in the role of James Bond was unimpressed. Towering over Stompanato and also a bodybuilder, his own formation from the Fountainbridge tenements of Edinburgh made a pointed weapon an irritating distraction. He reportedly bent back Stompanato's hand forcing him to drop the weapon. He then leveled him with a right hook prompting his assailant to flee the movie set.

The account still reads well decades later and may even be true.

Stompanato was immediately deported from the United Kingdom for weapon possession. The film was completed without further incident and released with modest acclaim. Several similar version remakes would follow. Lana Turner returned to the United States with a stalled career and more abuse at the hands of an enraged and humiliated Stompanato. Turner's fourteen-year-old daughter Cheryl Crane silenced his anger one evening.

On April 4, 1958 during yet another confrontation between

Turner and Stompanato, she impaled him fatally with a carving knife. She maintained at her trial that he was in the act of violently attacking her mother. A jury agreed and returned a verdict of justifiable homicide.

Not everyone applauded the decision. The Stompanato family filed a $7 million damage suit against Lana Turner. Mickey Cohen threatened Connery during his first filming visit to the Los Angeles area. Connery prudently lingered under the public radar briefly. During the 1960s, he emerged in films as *007*, a suave and worldly British secret agent.

Turner's career briefly resurged following the murder and a return to the public spotlight. The film industry has never been charitable to aging actresses and her roles steadily lessened. Her career lapsed into a forced semi-retirement. She died at the age of 74 in 1995.

Cheryl Crane's life followed a circuitous path after the murder. She published a book in 1988 detailing the trauma of living within her mother's turbulent household and her eventual emotional recovery following the trial. She ultimately relocated to Palm Springs with a stable partner and a less dramatic existence.

Johnny Stompanato
730 North Bedford Drive, Beverly Hills

PHOTO:
Lana Turner's home and murder site

The Kryptonite Curse That Felled Superman George Reeves

George Reeves became the speculated fourth victim of a curse that afflicted actors portraying the role of Clark Kent and Superman. His 1959 impulsive suicide would be followed forty-five years later by successor Christopher Reeve's ill fortune. A freak equestrian riding accident in 1995 left Reeve paralyzed from the neck down. Reeve died nine years later from heart failure attributed to his medical condition.

Reeves, like original film actor Kirk Alyn and Reeve was identified strongly with the role to the detriment of other acting aspirations. He was born as George Brewer on January 5, 1914 in Woolstock, Iowa to a couple on the verge of divorcing. Reeves followed his mother to Illinois and later California where she met and married Frank Bessolo. His stepfather adopted George as his own son and he changed his last name to Bessolo. His mother's fifteen-year marriage to Frank Bessolo ended in divorce with the couple separating while George was visiting relatives. Returning from his stay, his mother informed him that his stepfather had committed suicide. She lied to him. Several years later he discovered Bessolo was still alive.

Reeves began his acting studies in 1939 at the Pasadena Playhouse and was cast as red-haired Stuart Tarleton, one of Scarlett O'Hara's suitors in the classic film *Gone With The Wind*. Warner Brothers signed him to a studio contract and changed his professional name to *George Reeves*.

During his years with Warner Brothers and later Twentieth Century-Fox, Reeves appeared in numerous short films, westerns and forgettable dramas. He was drafted into the US Army in early 1943, but experienced no combat.

Instead he acted in military theatre productions and appeared in training films.

Discharged at the end of World War II, he returned to acting and again was cast in minor performance roles. His career break and ultimate noose came with his 1951 selection as Superman in a new television series *Adventures of Superman*. He was not the producer's first choice, but Kirk Alyn declined the role and many actors considered television a marginal medium with limited viewership.

The half-hour episodes were filmed on tight scheduling with two completed every six days. All of the first season's episodes were completed within 13 weeks during the summer. Cast members had very restrictive contracts preventing them from accepting other work that might interfere with the series. This effectively excluded Reeves from accepting major film work or extended Broadway theatre runs. As television viewership expanded, Reeves was able to earn money from public appearances.

Reeves national popularity as Superman enabled him leverage to demand a sizable contract increase in 1953. His ambitions leaned towards creating a new production company and television adventure series. He was never able to raise sufficient funding and his project was never realized. Throughout the balance of the decade, he continued his Superman role, even guest-appearing once on the *I Love Lucy* show. Although he found the role unchallenging and limiting, his financial situation depended upon it. At 45, Reeves' viable options for making a living had narrowed exclusively to appearing as Superman.

His personal life became messy. He had first married in 1940 and divorced ten years later. He was linked to a long-term affair with Toni Mannix, the wife of Eddie Mannix, general manager for Metro-Goldwyn-Mayer. Mannix was rumored to have organized crime ties. Their affair ended in 1958. Afterwards he announced his engagement to society fixture Leonore Lemmon stating that they would marry on June 19, 1959.

Four days before the wedding, they had a public dispute at a restaurant dinner. Both reportedly returned to Reeves' house with a third dinner companion. They were joined later by an intimate group of friends and neighbors. Reeves had retired earlier intent on sleep. The group's drinking and noise continued past midnight awakening a belligerent Reeves. He joined the group briefly, but returned upstairs to the bedroom in a foul mood.

His guests claimed they heard a single gunshot between 1:30 and 2:00 a.m. He was discovered with his naked body facing upwards on the bed with his feet on the floor. Police arrived within an hour, but had difficulty obtaining a clear account of the events due to the extreme inebriation of the group. The most consistent conclusion was that Reeves had shot himself due to his perception of a *failed career* and his inability to find roles that he wanted.

Not everyone was convinced of the suicide theory. His mother unsuccessfully attempted to have the case re-opened as a homicide. Questionable police findings cast suspicions of doubt. The fatal bullet was recovered from Reeves' bedroom ceiling and the shell casing under his body. Two additional bullets were embedded in the floor. All three had been fired from the Lugar pistol found next to his feet. No fingerprints were lifted from the gun and gunpowder residue was absent from Reeve's hand. There was no evidence of forced entry or that a second person was in the room. The County Coroner ruled his death a suicide.

George Reeves' mortal ambitions and subsequent depression became his personal kryptonite. Many actors have discovered typecasting as a limiting obstacle to professional diversity. For the ambitious but unsuccessful acting legions who've never enjoyed fame or steady employment, most would have gratefully accepted Reeves dilemma in a heartbeat.

George Reeves Residence
1579 Benedict Canyon Road, Beverly Hills

PHOTO: George Reeve's House

A Clueless Doctor and Lover Botch A Murder of Convenience

In 1959 at the age of 42, Raymond Bernard Finch had constructed a lucrative medical practice ornamented by professional prestige, an opulent West Covina residence with a South Hills Country Club membership and an attractive mistress half his age. She coincidentally was his secretary.

His carefully constructed façade had a singular vulnerability, his wife Barbara Finch. If she could prove adultery and divorce him, an eminent likelihood, financial ruin was almost certain. California's community property laws and the obligation of materially supporting their two children would be financially lethal.

His medical competence didn't extend into his personal affairs. He hatched a scheme with mistress Carole Tregoff to hire a Las Vegas based ex-con gigolo named John Patrick Cody to seduce and ensnare Barbara Finch into her own extra-marital affair. This liaison would enable the doctor to potentially countersue his wife for her own infidelity.

Tregoff was by then working in Las Vegas and handled the logistical details of the plan. The improbable seduction project was scrapped. A contract killing seemed more appealing. Cody assured the couple he was capable of the act.

He accepted Tregoff's down payment of $350 and a weekend roundtrip airline ticket to Los Angeles. He departed and returned as planned and assured Tregoff that his end of the transaction had been completed. He was paid the agreed upon balance of $850.

124

He neither visited nor killed Barbara Finch. Instead he'd spent the weekend lounging with one of his numerous girlfriends. Cody expressed astonishment with the revelation that Mrs. Finch remained amongst the living. His response: *I must have killed the wrong woman.* The fleeced but still credulous Tregoff paid him an additional two hundred dollars to complete the job. She would be disappointed once again.

Finch and Tregoff became even more desperate to rid the respectable doctor of his financially troublesome impediment towards bliss.

On the evening of July 8, 1959, the couple arrived at 10 p.m. to his empty house. Barbara drove into the garage an hour later. The impatient Finch confronted her as she exited her red Chrysler.

In the melee that followed, according to the Finch's maid at trial, the doctor pistol-whipped his 35-year-old wife and then shot her fatally in the back with a .38 caliber pistol as she attempted to flee via the driveway. He also slammed the maid's head against their garage wall in an unexplainable effort to stun her.

After the killing, Finch sprinted across the manicured country club golf course lawns. He stole two cars in the process of driving to Las Vegas. The next morning Tregoff joined him. She had viewed the entire murder and subsequent police arrival unseen and paralyzed behind a bougainvillea bush.

She drove all night confessing her first knowledge of Barbara's death arrived via a car radio newscast. She indicated that she relayed the news to Finch upon arrival.

He merely shrugged it off. She reportedly returned to work that morning. Finch was arrested that same day and charged with first-degree murder. Eleven days later, Tregoff was arrested as an accomplice.

In January 1960 at the Los Angeles County Courthouse, their spectacle trial played to a packed audience. The proceedings didn't disappoint especially during John Patrick Cody and Dr. Finch's testimony.

Cody freely admitted he had deceived the couple with his murder-for-hire swindle and typified himself as a *professional loafer*.

Finch recreated the fatal sequence of events by stating his wife had pulled a gun on him and then taken direct aim at Tregoff. When he intervened by grabbing and prying away the pistol, Barbara commenced to run down the driveway. As he attempted to toss the gun aside, he accidentally shot her between the shoulder blades severing an artery that stimulated her fatal bleeding.

His incredulous tale cast him as an unfortunate victim. He insisted that he telephoned an ambulance and his dying Barbara apologized for her hasty and imprudent actions. Before the ambulance could arrive, her pulse ceased. He realized that she had expired. As he wiped away a courtroom tear, his breaking voice returned to its normal buoyancy and further cross-examination continued. The only element lacing was an organ crescendo to accompany his melodramatic yarn.

A revealing question tested his fidelity towards Tregoff when posed to Finch on witness stand. He was asked if he had told *all* of his numerous former mistresses that he loved them. Nonplussed, the doctor responded *I think under the circumstances that would be routine.*

Carole Tregoff's ardor toward the surgeon had cooled significantly. She had rejected all of his letters and attempts at communication since their arrest. Her intention towards becoming a future Mrs. Finch had evolved into a more pragmatic priority towards self-preservation.

After eight days of deliberation, the jury was unable to concur on a verdict and a mistrial was declared. Two minority jury members were rumored to have resisted the Caucasian jurors' insistence on a murder conviction. Six months later, another deadlocked jury followed with the judge instructing the jury that they should disregard the testimony of both defendants.

A three-month trial followed in early 1961 minus the accompanying hysteria. Finch was convicted of first-degree murder and Tregoff second-degree. Both were sentenced to life imprisonment.

Life imprisonment has always seemed subjective when it comes to prison term lengths. In 1969, Tregoff was paroled, changed her name and reportedly found employment at a hospital in nearby Pasadena. She moved back to her former West Covina neighborhood and lived in obscurity.

Finch was released from prison two years later. He relocated to Missouri and established a family physician and surgical practice in the towns of El Dorado Springs and Bolivar between 1975-1985. He again moved his practice to Rancho Mirage, California where he died on May 15, 1995. He eventually remarried and had three subsequent children.

If one lesson emerged from this immoral saga, murder-for-hire is most efficiently conducted by true professionals.

Finch Murder Residence
2750 Lark Hill Drive, West Covina

PHOTO: Finch Residence

Geneva Ellroy: The Transference of Tragedy Into Literary Expression

Reading author James Ellroy's *My Dark Places* is an exercise in observing the lingering and consequential effects of an unsolved murder in the life of a survivor.

On the late evening of Saturday, June 21, 1958, Ellroy's mother, Geneva (Jean) was viciously strangled with a cotton cord and one of her stockings. She was dragged on asphalt and dumped in an acacia and ivy thicket. The location was a lane known as Kings Row, behind the Arroyo High School football stadium in El Monte. She was a redheaded 37-year-old divorcee and registered nurse.

Pearls from a broken necklace led to the body. According to newspaper accounts, she was disheveled in a torn blue dress with no undergarments. A navy blue coat covered the nude half of her lower body and one stocking was pulled down to her ankle. Her brassiere had been removed.

Her murder was the fourth committed in El Monte up to that point in 1958. Her killer was never identified. Unlike the other three homicides, which were followed by quick arrests, Ellroy's killing lacked substantive leads, motive and witnesses. Police sought for questioning an unidentified blonde woman with a ponytail. The two women had been sighted together the evening before at a local cocktail bar. Ellroy's car was located in the parking lot on the day following her murder.

The crime generated local coverage briefly, but the urgency behind the investigation withered.

For 10-year-old son James Ellroy, the consequences proved both devastating and pivotal towards the shaping of his personal and professional direction.

He candidly documented his adolescent and adult demons in his autobiography *My Dark Places*. The book traced the author's decent into depression, anti-social behavior, alcoholism and drug addition. He detailed much of his personal decline towards his mother's abrupt absence and the blunt trauma behind her death.

His own personal devastation eventually was productively channeled into writing. His globally popular crime novels included *The Black Dahlia*, *The Big Nowhere*, *LA Confidential* and *White Jazz*. Speculation is widespread that his writings about the Black Dahlia's (Elizabeth Short) unsolved murder may have been directly influenced by his own mother's less publicized killing.

My Dark Places documents his own research and successful effort to reopen his mother's cold case. The time lag, absence of remaining evidence and living references made the case irresolvable.

Jean Ellroy, like many divorcees of her era was stigmatized and obliged to seek dubious outlets for sexual partners. Her violation and death by presumably one of her partners would have generated minimal empathy. The pattern of personality disintegration by her son was not unusual in instance of violent killings.

The acacia thicket no longer remains. The dumping site is a uniformly paved and lined unassuming parking lot. For the three baseball coaches who discovered the body and one impressionable young man, the site would remain unforgettable. The three coaches, then middle-aged are since deceased. The ten-year-old boy remains permanently tainted.

Despite an unsatisfying solution due to the passage of time, one positive element emerged. Ellroy's skill of detailed writing has subsequently fascinated and educated readers into the intricacies behind criminal acts. His own personal agony was transcribed into a genuine voice.

His legacy of tragedy gifted a written expression of clarity.

Geneva Ellroy Killing:
Kings Row, Acacia thicket across from Arroyo High School Athletic Field

PHOTO:
Approximate location of Acacia thicket where Geneva Ellroy's body found

Marilyn Monroe: A Final Action Freezing Perpetual Fame

Marilyn Monroe's ascent to Hollywood stardom and her shocking death has become fodder for speculation for over fifty-five years. Monroe had just turned 36, but her career had begun to wane. Suddenly she was gone.

She had enjoyed a decade of success as one of the world's leading actresses, but her erratic behavior on her last two films had resulted in production problems and her being fired from the last one, *Something's Got to Give*. Most of the problems were traced to her being late to film sets and having trouble remembering her lines.

1961 had been a horrendous year for Monroe. In January, her third marriage to author Arthur Miller officially ended in divorce. She underwent surgeries for two health issues and reportedly spent four weeks under hospital care. Part of her stay was in a mental ward for depression. That same year, she would purchase her Spanish hacienda-style home in Brentwood.

Weeks preceding her demise, she was attempting to repair her reputation by giving interviews to high-profile and mass circulating magazines. Her last studio had publicly blamed her for sabotaging production and faking her mental health issues. Her emotional vulnerability was well documented based on her abusive past. Her dependencies on amphetamines, barbiturates and alcohol were unknown to the public but familiar issues within her inner circle. She remained publicly optimistic towards her future, but her internal torments and anxieties doggedly persisted.

She spent the final day of her life, Saturday August 4, 1962 at her home accompanied by her publicist, housekeeper, personal photographer and psychiatrist. Her housekeeper remained with her that evening to keep her company.

Monroe locked her bedroom door for privacy. She suffered from chronic insomnia, so sleeping pills were a normal component of her bedtime routine. At 3 a.m., her housekeeper noted that she appeared unresponsive when viewed through a window into her bedroom. Her psychiatrist was summoned and entered the room by breaking the window. She was discovered dead, nude and with a telephone receiver in her hand.

When the details of her death were published, speculation followed immediately as to whom her call was intended to. Conspiracy theories arose suggesting murder and a subsequent cover-up. She had been linked romantically to affairs with President John F. Kennedy and his brother Robert, mobster Sam Giancana and even labor union leader Jimmy Hoffa.

The Los Angeles County Coroner ruled her death a *probable suicide* based on the quantity (40+) of barbiturates she has ingested. No published evidence of foul play was ever revealed. This lack of evidence has never ceased imaginative recreations regarding her death.

In a cul-de-sac surrounded by renovated and multi-leveled houses, Marilyn's modest bungalow remains as a preserved time capsule behind protective gated walls. Like its owner, perceptions are stilled and frozen. Within the general public's imagination, Marilyn Monroe shouldn't be allowed to age gracefully. The banal facts behind her desperate drug overdose appear too simplistic to accept. Entertainment icons are scarcely humanized and even in death, contributing factors are magnified.

Misunderstood during her era, she would find solace and equilibrium even more elusive today with the aggressive intrusions of social media.

Marilyn Monroe's Residence
12305 Fifth Helena Drive, Los Angeles

The Abrupt Departure of a Soul Music Legend In His Prime

In the winter of 1964, Sam Cooke was an established international star enthroned atop the popular music industry. Between 1957 and 1964, he had registered thirty American top 40 hits. His most renowned compositions and distinctive renditions of *You Send Me*, *Cupid*, *Wonderful World*, *Chain Gang* and *Twistin' the Night Away* still stir emotional sensibilities.

His pioneering publishing, business acumen and performance contributions directly influenced the rise and sustainability of soul music legends Aretha Franklin, Bobby Womack, Al Green, Stevie Wonder, Marvin Gaye, Billy Preston, Curtis Mayfield, Otis Redding and James Brown.

In his prime at 33, this handsome and charismatic performer had not only established an enduring legacy, but also possessed the ambition, talent and capacity to distance and surpass his contemporaries. He was prolifically creative, inspired and directly involved in every aspect of his production arrangements.

By late 1964, he was twice married and once divorced. He had three children by his second wife although one had died at the age of two.

On the evening of December 11, 1964, Cooke attended a Los Angeles nightclub and shared time with Elisa Boyer who he'd met there. Instead of escorting her home as she claimed to have repeatedly requested, he checked both of them into the seamy Hacienda Motel on South Figueroa Street. The property has varied minimally over the ensuing decades with the exception of name and ownership changes.

Varied accounts and chronologies of events have differed over each participant's role, intent and fault in the subsequent tragedy. Each version has stimulated dispute and even more questions.

Boyer's versions indicated that upon his use of the bathroom to take a shower, she accidentally grabbed some of his intermingled clothing with hers while attempting a hasty flight from the property. She testified at a preliminary inquest, she feared Cooke was intent on raping her. Other versions suggest that she had deliberately enticed him to the motel to steal his wallet and belongings.

Cooke reportedly raced furiously down the staircase into the manager's office apparently wearing only a sports coat and his shoes. He assumed that Boyer was hiding in the office despite manager Bertha Franklin's denials. Franklin claimed Cooke exhibited intimidating and violent behavior that escalated into an ensuing verbal and physical struggle. Franklin retrieved a shotgun from the back and mortally shot Cooke dead in the torso.

Her claim of self-defense and Boyer's corroboration of events resulted in an inquest ruling of *justifiable homicide*. Suspicions remain over inconsistencies and the credibility of the testimony, particularly amongst family members and associates closest to Cooke. Subsequent evidence has not shed any new insight into the events.

What becomes obvious is that Sam Cooke was in the wrong location, with the wrong person at the wrong time.

His death became yet another tragic creative force that ending prematurely. We will never know what beauty he may have further revealed.

Sam Cooke Shooting:
Former Hacienda Motel, 9137 South Figueroa, Los Angeles

Lenny Bruce: An Iconic Casualty Drowned By An Unrelenting Current

Lenny Bruce altered the perception of stand-up comedy perhaps more than any practitioner and it likely cost him his life at the premature age of 40. He cultivated virgin performance territory with his rapid fire and freestyle version of delivery that was less about being clownish, than provocation, shock and pushing an audience to think. His material stressed social commentary on politics, religion, sex and he laced it liberally with satire and profanity.

No subject remained taboo from Bruce's scathing attacks and the flawed establishment he skewered ultimately fought back viciously. He did not invent stand-up comedy, but he opted to shatter perceived stereotypes. His audience sometimes chaffed and squirmed when he refused to back down from uncomfortable material. He was different and many considered his perspective genius.

Bruce reluctantly led a corps of counterculture era comedians that redefined humor nearly casting the traditional scripted setup and punchline format into irrelevance. There was a steep price for his pioneering. He was first arrested on October 4, 1961 at the *Jazz Workshop* in San Francisco for referencing popular sexual and genital slang. Rather than tame his act, Bruce expanded this material over his remaining years resulting in further obscenity arrests following performances. His arrest in London resulted in his prohibition from returning to the United Kingdom. His comedy routines documented his encounters with police and the judicial system. These monologues extended into furious rants and tirades sprayed upon his audience. His first legal conviction was in 1964.

Bruce frequently polarized his audience base. For many, he

represented a must-see impending train wreck. As his emotional and mental health fluctuated erratically, he rarely disappointed. The complexity and layered tone of his material seemed too raw and far-sighted for its era. Little of his content has been passed down. He was essentially blacklisted from television appearances and only released four recording albums. His stream of consciousness approach might be emulated by comic successors, but impossibly duplicated due to its intensely personal nature.

Born Leonard Alfred Schneider in Mineola, New York, Bruce joined the Navy at the age of 16 in 1942 and was involved in active fighting during World War II off the coast of Italy. He was given an *undesirable discharge* in July 1945 after reportedly defiantly convincing his ship's medical officer that he was experiencing homosexual urges. He later fought and succeeded in having his discharge modified to *Under Honorable Conditions*.

Following the war, Bruce steadily commenced his professional comic trajectory appearing regularly and cultivating a following from the smallest dives into the most prestigious venues then available to itinerant comics. His material evolved into controversial and was often typified as *sick*, *irreverent* and *uncomfortable*.

Throughout the final decade of his life, Bruce's drug addiction worsened. His addictions included a decimating stream of meth, amphetamines and heroin. Rather than treat his chemical dependency, he simply incorporated his experiences into his performance repertoire. The arrests, cancelled performances and court appearances were steadily eroding his stability and financial livelihood. Few clubs would book him despite his fame for fear of arrest for violating obscenity laws. Disaster seemed always eminent. The end was swiftly abrupt. Few close observers were astonished when Bruce overdosed on morphine on August 3, 1966 in his Hollywood Hills residence. He was discovered naked on a floor with a syringe and burned bottle cap nearby accompanied by other drug paraphernalia.

He was subsequently eulogized and later canonized as a landmark spokesperson for freedom of speech rights.

It is difficult to accurately measure the impact of Lenny Bruce's legacy. Upon his storming and widening the portals of comic expression, the breach enabled generations of *difficult to classify* comedians a livelihood.

Mediocre stand up content has likewise followed. A sickening flow of sexist, racist and drug-obsessed content has established its presence as mainstream humor. This vulgarity masquerades as insightful social commentary. The simple minded are amused by the excess and stench. This is not the fault of Lenny Bruce. His material was never targeted for simpletons.

Lenny Bruce's Residence:
8825 West Hollywood Boulevard, Los Angeles 90069

PHOTO: Entrance to Lenny Bruce Residence

Senator Robert F. Kennedy: The Assassination of Hope

Robert F. Kennedy represented many diverse inspiring images to Americans. Long before the term *Hope* was employed by Barrack Obama's initial presidential campaign, Kennedy epitomized hope and change for societies disenfranchised.

America in June 1968 had arrived at a crossroads. Amidst the contagious rebellion against an increasingly unpopular war in Vietnam and a general malaise within American culture, Kennedy represented a sense of coherent dignity and clarity.

Some of his appeal may have been rooted by the high public regard for the Kennedy family name. Robert Kennedy was unmistakably unique. He was often reviled as much as admired for his blunt candor.

He was firmly against the Vietnam War, a military conflict his presidential brother John had escalated while in office. Serving in the Kennedy administration as the United States Attorney General, he dealt with controversial Civil Rights issues and exposed corruption within organized labor.

He completed the majority of his term under a hostile presidential successor Lyndon Johnson before resigning to run for the U.S. Senate. He was successfully elected by the State of New York and assumed office in 1965.

During his tenure in the Senate, Kennedy became an outspoken advocate of Israel. His unwavering support had been formulated during a residence in the country in his early twenties and a genuine admiration of the Jewish inhabitants.

The Presidential election of 1968 became an alternating shift of preferences within Kennedy's Democratic Party. President Lyndon Johnson's popularity suffered severely due his Vietnam War policies and the magnitude of social unrest. To Johnson's credit, he introduced more anti-poverty and anti-discrimination legislation than any predecessor or successor. Johnson obstinacy imagined he could salvage victory in an unwinnable and demoralizing war.

His narrow victory in the New Hampshire primary against anti-war candidate, Minnesota Senator Eugene McCarthy convinced him of his electable vulnerability

Following the primary, he made a national speech indicating he would no longer seek re-election. This announcement left the Democratic field wide open.

One month following his announcement, Vice-President Hubert Humphrey, also from Minnesota, declared his candidacy. He did not enter any primaries. His status as front-runner was based on previously declared delegates whose commitments were not permanently binding.

McCarthy's initial campaign success was based on his open opposition to the Vietnam War and efforts to empower younger voters. Kennedy delayed his entry into the race until after the New Hampshire primary on March 16. He immediately seized popular momentum. McCarthy's appeal began to subside. With Humphrey absent from the primary ballots, Kennedy ran exclusively against McCarthy and captured the majority of the primaries.

On April 4th, Civil Rights leader Martin Luther King was assassinated in Memphis and a stewing cauldron of racial turmoil and violence erupted nationally. The United States was in tumult and experiencing a collective disillusionment towards central leadership. A sense of change appeared necessary. Opposing perspectives became polarized and debate antagonistic. In the eyes of many, the election of Robert Kennedy represented the potential for fulfillment of the idealistic and interrupted dreams of his assassinated brother.

Views of history can effortlessly lapse into a speculation sport. Probable outcomes are not tested by actual events. Was Robert Kennedy the calming influence America required? Would the subsequent trajectory of American history been altered? We will never know.

On June 4, 1968, Robert Kennedy narrowly won the California primary over Eugene McCarthy. At that moment, he ranked second to Humphrey in delegates for the Democratic nomination.

His delegate momentum surge had clearly ascended him on an accelerated course to overtake the front-runner. That evening signified the final influence either McCarthy or Kennedy would exert on the Democratic Party. McCarthy's popularity never regained popular traction. Kennedy was shot to death.

Shortly after midnight, four hours after the California polls had closed, Kennedy addressed his campaign supporters in the Ambassador Hotel's Embassy Ballroom located in the mid-Wilshire district of Los Angeles. His mood was optimistic and jubilant. Kennedy was on target to gain the nomination and very likely the presidency.

During that era, the government provided secret service protection for incumbent presidents but not declared candidates. Kennedy's security force consisted of a former

FBI agent and several professional athletes serving as unofficial bodyguards.

The chaos following his victory speech created media deadline complications due to the late hour. Kennedy was originally scheduled to meet with an additional group of supporters in another section of the hotel, Instead, he was escorted through a hotel kitchen pantry to an awaiting press conference.

The crowd hemmed in Kennedy as he threaded through the kitchen while shaking hands en route. From the crevices of a narrow passageway, Sirhan Sirhan, a 24-year-old Palestinian national emerged and began firing a .22 caliber revolver into a distracted Kennedy and his entourage.

He shot Kennedy three times. He wounded five others and was finally wrestled to the ground and struck repeatedly by Kennedy's protective guards.

Kennedy did not die immediately. He reportedly asked about the welfare of the other victims before slipping into unconsciousness. He lingered for 26 hours before finally expiring. One of the bullets had entered behind his right ear and dispersed fragments through his brain. He was only 42-years-old.

Speculation began immediately towards the killing being a calculated conspiracy. It remains unclear how Sirhan anticipated the divergent routing through the kitchen passage.

Initially, Sirhan's strong anti-Zionist beliefs were identified as the obsession behind the killing. A purportedly discovered diary of Sirhan's confirmed his resolution to kill Kennedy. In subsequent rambling interviews, Sirhan has since blamed brainwashing tactics and memory loss for his inability to pinpoint why he was present at the Ambassador Hotel that fateful evening. He remains incarcerated at the RJ Donovan Correctional Facility in San Diego awaiting a much-welcomed demise by many.

His elimination of a potential history transformer resulted in profound domestic and international consequences. The August Democratic Convention in Chicago resulted in combative protests. Hubert Humphrey emerged from the chaos nominated by the party, but tainted. Former Vice-President Richard Nixon secured the uncontested Republican nomination and handily defeated Humphrey in the national election. He ran on a campaign platform promising to restore law and order.

Both candidates sidestepped the Vietnam War issue during campaigning. Nixon ultimately signed a peace treaty four years later ingloriously ending the conflict. Despite several notable foreign policy achievements, he would self-destruct his own legacy through the Watergate cover-up scandal.

The morale of Americans would stagnate through an extended period of economic woe and international military conflicts. Idealists suggest that Kennedy's leadership may have avoided the accompanying dissatisfaction.

The Ambassador Hotel ceased hospitality operations in 1989, but remained open for filming and private events. During 2005, the majority of the building was demolished leaving only the annex that housed the hotel entrance, shipping arcade, coffee shop and a portion of the *Cocoanut Grove Nightclub*. The kitchen pantry area, the site of the shooting was included in the demolition.

The Central Los Angeles New Learning Center, along with

the Robert F. Kennedy Inspiration Park was built on the Ambassador grounds. An extensive peace memorial adorns the Wilshire Boulevard frontage. The metal memorials are testimonies to peace but cannot adequately capture the loss and significance of the promise Kennedy once offered.

Robert Kennedy briefly represented the same progressive change and options his brother John symbolized for so many. It is impossible to conclude whether a divided nation had the capacity to heal immediately amidst such era of rupture. It is equally debatable that our nation, with its entrenched two-party system influenced by special interest monies, may ever fully recover onto a single united course.

Senator Robert F. Kennedy Killing:
Kitchen Pantry in the Former Ambassador Hotel, 3400 Wilshire Boulevard, Los Angeles

PHOTOS:
Former site of the Ambassador Hotel and Peace Memorial

148

Ramon Novarro: The Gruesome Torture of a Closeted Screen Idol

Ramon Novarro entered the infant silent film industry in 1917 playing small roles. By 1923, his roles became more prominent and he was touted as a rival to Rudolph Valentino as the screen's dominant *Latin Lover*. Upon Valentino's abrupt death in 1926, he ascended to an elite level eclipsed only by actor John Gilbert.

He was considered one of the great romantic lead actors appearing and seducing leading actresses such as Joan Crawford, Norma Shearer, Greta Garbo, Myrna Loy and Lupe Velez. He successfully made the transition into speaking parts with talking films but MGM studios did not renew his contract when it expired in 1935. He continued with minor inconsequential roles into the 1960s as his fame receded.

Novarro was born Jose Ramon Gil Samaniego to a well respected family who had emigrated from Durango, Mexico to Los Angeles in 1913 to escape a revolution in their country. His ancestry was traced back to the small Castilian town of Burgos.

He was one of thirteen children from a devout Roman Catholic family. Three of his sisters became nuns. His Catholic background created troubling conflicts with his lifestyle. His screen image as a dashing ladies man was fabricated. His closet homosexuality, while not novel in the film industry, traumatized him and influenced a directly attributed alcoholism.

He invested wisely in a Hollywood Hills residence, designed in 1927 by Lloyd Wright, the son of his more renowned architect father. He maintained a comfortable lifestyle with his former earnings. The man and his legacy became largely forgotten until his violent death.

Novarro became a frail and lonely alcoholic. On October 30, 1968, he hired two brothers, Paul and Tom Ferguson, aged 22 and 17, from a sex agency for services. What transpired that evening involved a severe beating administered by the brothers to Novarro when he failed to provide $5,000 presumed to be hidden on the premises. Novarro died by asphyxiation from his own blood.

The brothers were arrested and convicted to extended prison terms, but released on probation during the mid-1970s. Each would return to prison for a variety of offenses. Tom Ferguson committed suicide in 2005. Paul Ferguson is currently interned at the Crossroads Correction Center in Cameron, Missouri due to a 1989 conviction for rape and sodomy. An online published notice by a Missouri television station indicated that Ferguson was killed during a fight with his cellmate on August 17, 2018. Official confirmation has been impossible to obtain.

The disclosure of alternative sexual orientations amongst leading male actors has significantly evolved within mainstream cinema. Acceptance hasn't become universal. Novarro was rightfully protective of his reputation and public legacy. The ultimate selection of his paid companionship proved fatal.

Ramon Novarro Residence:
3110 Laurel Canyon Boulevard, Studio City

PHOTO:
Entrance to Roman Novarro's residence

Charles Manson: Removing the Myths Behind an Iconic Serial Killer

More publications, websites, and editorial space have been devoted towards Charles Manson, his cult followers and their subsequent atrocities than any comparative serial killer. Yet comparisons become truly scarce since Manson did not empty a single cartridge or physically kill any of his victims.

Instead, Manson manipulated a raggedy band of followers into murdering at least nine victims and potentially more. In particular, they were responsible for seven gruesome killings within a two-day spree in August 1969. These acts and the subsequent trial proceedings introduced the cult into public infamy.

Manson's techniques were neither novel nor inventive. An avowed racist, he embraced a self-perceived mantra of apocryphal killer ushering in a prophetic American racial Apocalypse. He erroneously envisioned that his planned killings would initiate class warfare motivated by race that would forever sever the American class and social hierarchy. His band of mesmerized puppets rarely exceeded two-dozen members. Yet an informal admiration base has curiously evolved since his incarceration if solely by distant and abstract adoration.

Amidst his own philosophical rants, he plagiarized lyrics from the Beatle's macabre *Helter Skelter* song, spouted revolutionary rhetoric common for the era and enforced subservience with tactical brainwashing techniques. These tactics included isolation, starvation, sexual and excessive drug dependence.

Over a progression of nearly three intense years, he

assembled a young, disenchanted and predominantly female follower base that bent obediently to his will. They viewed him as a magnetic messiah figure. His self-assured propaganda played well to impressionable minds seeking direction amidst an age of turmoil and dissension. His charade has been thoroughly documented by cult members, commentators and countless portrayals. Yet as with many of the icons of the 1960s protest era, he continues to fascinate fresh generations of spectators.

A candid appraisal of Charles Manson's activities would confirm that in a leadership role, a complete role reversal of his earlier past, he was able to assert dominance and submissive consent to weaker minds and temperaments. Without boundaries of morality or restraint, evil consequences typically take root.

But who is and was Charles Manson? Cloistered from the scrutiny of public expression, social and traditional media exposure, his true identify and character has been misrepresented into a toxic mythology. Why does there exist a continued fascination towards a lifelong habitual criminal and failure?

Manson was born in November 1932 and his itinerant father never identified. His mother and uncle were convicted of robbing a service station in 1939. He lived with another aunt and uncle in West Virginia during their internment. Upon her 1942 release and parole, he accompanied her as they drifted together throughout Midwest boarding houses. Soon they separated as his mother proved no more capable of raising a son than he adhering to a traditional upbringing.

He bounced around residences throughout Indiana, Utah, Ohio, Washington State and D.C, Virginia, and Texas. His random existence was accompanied solely by the certainty that he would always find legal entanglements.

A sequence of petty and minor felonies followed including burglaries, armed robberies, sodomy, pimping, and car theft throughout his next twenty-five years. His perpetual criminality was consistent with his mundane anti-social fueled conduct. The miniscule accomplishments he had accumulated and squandered had scarcely prepared him for the infamous attention he would later acquire.

Charles Manson was briefly married twice, divorced and the father of four documented children. Each has eluded public exposure. He likely played a nonexistent role in their upbringing with his transience and incarcerations.

When he was arraigned in 1969 for murder conspiracy, he was identified as an unemployed former convict who had spent the majority of his life in correctional institutions. He had been an unsuccessful singer and songwriter on the external fringe of the Los Angeles music industry chiefly due to chance encounters with insiders by women within his cult.

His twisted charisma, which ultimately influenced murder without remorse or hesitation made him unique. More likely, the timing, location, eminence of certain victims and savagery of the killings set him further apart. In context, the timing of his most known seven slayings was committed during a zenith of social turmoil.

Between 1968-69, the Vietnam War raged uncontrollably and university campus became protest vortexes. Violent racial clashes were erupting. Unresolved serial killings were rampant. The Soviet Union had crushed a nationalist uprising in Prague. Two of the most calming influences,

Martin Luther King and Robert Kennedy had been assassinated. A perception and belief confirming society's imminent implosion was not unfounded.

Manson offered no solutions. His certainty, paranoia and tirades appealed to submissive individuals seeking sanctuary from reality.

It is imperative to separate man from myth to understand a homicidal motivator. Charles Manson, over time and distance, merits no more introspection and insight than any other manipulative mass murderer.

The homicides that Manson was considered legally accountable for included:

His assistance with Bobby Beausoleil regarding the July 1969 knifing and slaying of Gary Hinman over a money dispute. Manson reportedly sliced off Hinman's left earlobe with a sword two days before the killing. Cult members Mary Brunner and Susan Atkins accompanied Beausoleil and reportedly took turns smothering Hinman after his initial stabbing.

Beausoleil was convicted of murder and condemned to life imprisonment. He is currently serving his sentence at the California State Prison Solano in Vacaville following several years in the Oregon State Penitentiary. On his 19th application following 18 refusals, a California parole board recommended that Beausoleil be released from prison. Their recommendation is currently before California Governor Gavin Newsome for review.

Mary Brunner served 6 1/2 years at the California Institute for Women before her release. Susan Atkins served 38 years of her sentence at the California Institute for Women before dying in 2009 of brain cancer.

On the evening of August 8, 1969 cult members Charles *Tex* Watson, Susan Atkins, Linda Kasabian and Patricia Krenwinkel were instructed to destroy the residents of an elevated property located on Cielo Drive in Beverly Hills. A prior tenant of the property had been record producer Terry Melcher, the son of actress Doris Day who had briefly shown interest in Manson's music. Manson felt slighted when Melcher evaded offering him a contract and had lost interest in his talents.

It has been reported that Manson knew Melcher was no longer living on the premises, so the reason behind his selection remains unclear. Some cult members suggested that the dwelling represented to him an *establishment* that would neither accept him as a person or his genius. Motion picture director Roman Polanski and his wife, actress Sharon Tate were leasing the residence.

The four cult members parked their vehicle at the lower base of Cielo Drive. Kasabian was the driver and ultimately became the lookout. The group walked up the access road to the house's entrance gate. The upper stretch of Cielo resembles an extended driveway to one of the lower households when crossing lower Cielo Drive. It is easy to overlook for someone unfamiliar with the street. Signage is absent indicating the upper tier of the street. Manson had visited the property previously seeking Melcher, so he was familiar with this confusing aspect of the layout.

The house featured extended rancho styling architecture with a phenomenal view of the Hollywood basin. A modest wood shingled gate and fence were the sole barriers to access. The fence sloped up a hillside. The group scaled the modest five-foot fence shortly around midnight without detection.

To their surprise and chagrin, 17-year old Steven Parent, a friend of the live-in groundskeeper, William Garretson was exiting the property simultaneously in his father's car via the electronic gate. Watson emerged from the shadows and confronted Parent. Despite his pleas for mercy, Watson callously slashed the watch off of Parent's wrist and shot him four times in rapid succession.

The group entered the house where the Sharon Tate and her guests were retiring for the evening in separate quarters. The subsequent mayhem and executions by excessive stabbings and shootings created a horrific carnage. The excess was due to their inexperience and incompetence. None were hardened convicts. Instead, each was simply acting on blind compliance to Manson's instructions.

Polanski was overseas filming during the massacre but his wife Sharon Tate, eight and a half months pregnant, became the most prominent victim. Others fatalities included Jay Sebring, a noted hairstylist, Abigail Folger, heiress to the Folger coffee fortune and a writer, Wojciech Frykowski. The killings were graphically detailed in print. With the premises presumably insulated by security devices, the public terror was heightened. The groundskeeper Garretson claimed that he heard nothing from his detached residence. Any personal curiosity exhibited by him or one of the neighbors over the noise would have added to the casualty list.

The former Cielo Drive structure has since been razed and reconstructed into a sprawling multi-level Mediterranean style mansion. The present colossus mirrors reconstruction trends prevalent amongst affluent Beverly Hills real estate.

Security protection has been enhanced and any vestige of the former structure is left to the imagination of the viewer.

Manson was displeased by the group's careless handiwork and accompanied the same four along with Leslie Van Houten and Steve Grogan to orchestrate another execution the following evening. Manson selected the home of supermarket executive Leno LaBianca and his wife Rosemary, a dress shop co-owner living in the Los Feliz sector to rectify the previous evenings debacle. He apparently decided on their residence because he had attended a party next door the previous year. Once again the house was located atop an elevated driveway. The group surprised the couple sleeping in separate rooms.

Both were bound and then repeatedly stabbed. Once again, the slaughter was brutal and planning equally inept even with their leader present. No evidence directly linked Manson with physically stabbing either victim.

Manson proved no more proficient at planning murder than evading capture. Initially, despite the amateurish sanitizing of the crime scene, serious leads or motives did not materialize for each apparent senseless killing. The police had not yet linked the two murders as directly related. Manson's cult lived isolated and significantly below suspicion inhabiting a former San Fernando Valley movie production complex called Spahn Ranch in the hills above Chatsworth.

The group's anonymity would soon be exposed…but not as murder suspects. On August 16, the Los Angeles Police Department raided their compound and arrested all 26 residents as suspects in an auto theft ring. Weapons were seized during the raid, but because the text of the warrant was misdated, the group was released from custody.

Manson suspected that Donald *Shorty* Shea, a ranch hand had assisted in setting up the raid hoping to evict the cult off of the property. Revenge was immediate. Three group members Bruce Davis, Tex Watson and Steve Grogan murdered Shea. His body was rumored to be dismembered, but in 1977, Grogan drew authorities a map of the cadaver's location where it was discovered intact. He was released from prison in 1985 and remains the sole cult member convicted of murder to be paroled. Bruce Davis is currently interned at the California Men's Colony Prison in San Luis Obispo. He has been approved for parole on five occasions, but denied each time by successive California governors.

Following Shea's murder, the cult relocated to Barker Ranch in even more remote Death Valley. Short on credible suspects, investigators began recognizing the similarities between each execution pointing towards the identical culprits. Informants detailed linkages directly to Manson's collective.

In October of 1969, the majority of the group members were arrested at the Barker Ranch. Persistent rumors of additional killings and desert burials abounded during that stretch. Bodies have never been unearthed.

Tex Watson had taken flight back to Texas after assisting with Shea's murder. Like Manson had repeatedly attempted during his deranged life, he sought to reinvent his personality with a respectable haircut and more conventional lifestyle. He was arrested in late November 1970 and fought extradition for nine months. He would be tried separately from the other suspects for this reason.

Arriving back in California several months after the group's conviction, Watson pathetically feigned mental illness by attempting to regress into a fetal state, refusing to talk or eat and shedding 55 pounds. His performance proved unsuccessful, as he was declared sane and fit for trial after a 90-day observation period at Atascadero State Hospital.

Patricia Krenwinkel had also relocated back to her native Alabama after her father had bailed her out of jail following the second arrest. She was extradited back to California to stand trial with the other principals.

The nine-month trial began in July 1970 with extensive global media coverage. Manson, coveting the performance spotlight, shaved off his hair completely and carving an X prominently on his forehead for theatrical effect claiming he was Satan's reincarnation. Years later, he would modify the simple cross into a swastika which still remains embedded.

A few of his female admirers would replicate his appearance. Some of the female defendants appeared blissfully absent and smiled sheepishly on camera. They appeared unconcerned towards the gravity or consequences of their actions. Viewers were appalled by their indifference. Despite their collective theatre, the magnitude of their monstrous acts sobered the jury. The seven-month trial resulted in Manson, Atkins, Krenwinkel and Van Houten being condemned to death. When Tex Watson was finally able to stand trial in October 1971, he was convicted in two weeks on seven counts of first-degree murder and condemned to death.

A curious aside to the proceedings was the abrupt disappearance of defense attorney Ronald Hughes representing Leslie Van Houten. He vanished while on a camping trip during a ten-day recess from the Tate-

LaBianca murder trial in November 1970. His body was found four months later but the cause of death was undeterminable. Many suspected that cult members murdered Hughes as an act of retaliation for his verbal disagreements with Charles Manson over defense strategies.

When the death penalty was briefly abolished in California in 1972, each of the prisoner's sentences was commuted to life in prison.

Initially incarcerated at San Quentin on death row with Watson, Manson was transferred to Folsom Prison and then the California Medical Facility at Vacaville. Manson was returned twice to each location and spent time in Pelican Bay State Prison and Corcoran State Penitentiary (twice). He was attacked twice, once by a member of the Aryan Brotherhood, a white supremacy gang and on another occasion by a Hare Krishna resulting in severe burns. Even the celebrity incarcerated face risks from peers seeking reputations. He was disciplined while imprisoned on multiple occasions.

He granted four national television interviews during the 1980s. Each appearance merely reinforced his profound psychosis, paranoia and need to be permanently separated from society. Since those public exposures, Manson remained isolated, stoic, and resigned to his damnation. He allowed his supporters, detractors and biographers to construct his personal mythology absent of personal contribution. His psychotically penetrating stares, public posturing acts and absolute lack of contrition have distanced him from any possibility of society's forgiveness. He would have been incapable of being admitted back. Death became his sole release on November 19, 2017 from cardiac arrest resulting from respiratory failure and colon

161

cancer.

Upon his death, three individuals filed formal claims stating their intention to take possession of Manson's remains and personal effects. No judicial decision has yet been rendered on the outcome.

Despite or *because* of his association with evil, numerous disenfranchised fringe individuals and groups have adopted his personage as their symbolic patron. The atrocities he was responsible for are distantly removed from the headlines. He has been erroneously linked as a folk hero outlaw and example of independent alternative living outside of the constraints of society.

In truth, he was marginally more than a bombastic, barbaric criminal with a self-absorbed personality. His proponents lionized him from afar because intimate inspection would have proven disillusioning.

His apocalyptic visions were as vacant as his hypnotically drugged follower's eyes and the grandiose legacy he envisioned. Despite post-incarceration pleura of often flattering music, books, television and motion picture portrayals, he consistently proved himself mediocre and incapable of remorse or humanity. Only the weak-willed and similarly deluded could and did mourn his death.

Charles Tex Watson is currently imprisoned at the R. J. Donovan Correctional Facility in San Diego following a stint at the Mule Creek State Prison in Ione. Patricia Krenwinkel and Leslie Van Houten are interned at the California Institution for Women in Corona. All have been denied parole on multiple occasions.

Linda Kasabian served no jail time as she received

immunity in exchange for her damaging testimony against the cult. She evaded public scrutiny by returning to the east coast but was arrested in a Washington State drug raid in 1996. She publicly resurfaced in a 2009 interview with *The Guardian* newspaper. The article repeated known facts regarding the killings and she reinforced her diminutive role in their commission. A 2017 newspaper article stated her residence as Tacoma.

In examining the wreckage and catastrophe of so many wasted young lives, it becomes difficult to illuminate even a penlight of brightness amidst the darkness. The convicted murderers, with the exception of Manson, became generally model and compliant prisoners as one might assume of subservient personalities.

Each has uniquely channeled their personal misfortune into guidance and positive counseling towards their fellow inmates. Some have earned college degrees online and have become promoters of prison literary, drug and alcoholic rehabilitation programs. A few publicly espoused religious conversions in their lives and established ministries. Each has repeatedly expressed remorse and begged forgiveness for their actions.

Their positive prison activities have doubtlessly exceeded any contribution they may have ultimately offered had they been released to society. They may or may not be granted liberty one day, but without exception, it will be at an advanced age.

An aging but recollecting society, the victim's families and acquaintances will probably never fully forgive them. Perhaps God ultimately will.

Roman Polanski and Sharon Tate's leased mansion:
10050 Cielo Drive, Beverly Hills
Leno and Rosemary LaBianca: 3301 Waverly Drive, Los
Angeles
Spahn Ranch: Located in the hills between Northridge and
Simi Valley

PHOTOS:
Upper Cielo Drive, Rebuilt Entrance Gate (Where Steven
Parent Was Slain), Walkway Leading Up to the Mansion,
Rebuilt Mansion Perched on the Summit and Driveway
Leading up to the LaBianca Residence.

The Deadliest Firefight in California Highway Patrol History

Every time a law enforcement officer pulls a vehicle over for a traffic infraction, the potential for danger becomes the scariest part of their job. There are never routine stops absent of this fear.

The worst-case scenario for the California Highway Patrol (CHP) occurred on April 5, 1970, when two heavily armed criminals engaged officers in a deadly shootout at a Newhall restaurant parking lot.

Bobby Davis, 27, and Jack Twinning, 35, were career criminals with extended histories of violent felonies. Twinning had the dubious distinction of having spent five years in Alcatraz, during which he killed another prisoner in self-defense. The pair had met in jail. Both had been recently released from prison and Davis was on parole status in Houston.

Unsuccessful in finding legitimate jobs, they drove together from Houston to Sacramento, returning to more comfortable employment, robbing banks. They were unsuccessful. They headed to southern California and rented an apartment together in Long Beach.

En route, they observed construction in the mountainous Grapevine section near Gorman on US Interstate 5. They anticipated stealing explosives from the site for use in future bank robberies and particular armored cars.

On the evening of April 5th, the two initiated their plan to return to the construction site armed with handguns, rifles and shotguns. Davis dropped Twinning off near the site with the intention of stealing the explosives. Davis

167

inexplicably made a U-turn across the highway median, barely avoiding another vehicle heading southbound.

The driver of the near miss yelled at Davis and both vehicles pulled off to the side of the road. In the course of their heated exchange, Davis pulled out a firearm. The other driver, a military serviceman convinced the dull-witted Davis that CHP officers were nearby. Davis drove off and picked up Twinning. The driver telephoned the incident to the nearby highway patrol station complete with a description of Davis and his vehicle.

Several minutes later, CHP squad car partners Walt Frago and Roger Gore spotted the distinctive red Pontiac near Castaic and followed it. Another patrol car with Officers James Pence and George Alleyn awaited the two vehicles in nearby Valencia as back up.

The tailing officers instructed Davis to pull over at a freeway exit that today leads to the Six Flags Magic Mountain theme park and into a restaurant parking lot. The lot remains in operation today under a different eating establishment. The officers ordered the pair to exit their vehicle. Complying, Davis left his driver's seat and walked to the front hood of his car where Gore began to search him.

Frago approached the passenger side armed with a shotgun, but tilted airborne. Twinning exited the passenger seat and immediately fired upon Frago with two shots from his .28 revolver killing him instantly. Gore drew his service revolver and attempted to return fire. He had lost track of Davis adjacent to him. Davis yanked a .38 Special from his waistband and fired two lethal shots into Gore at close range.

Shortly after the initial exchange, Officers Alleyn and Pence arrived and initiated a subsequent firefight. The ensuing gun battle between the two sides resulted in the deaths of Pence and Alleyn who were badly outgunned. Twinning was superficially wounded. Gary Kness, a former U.S. Marine driving to work, entered the fray using one of the fallen officer's pistols against the perpetrators. A fragment from one of his bullets lodged in Davis's chest. Out of ammunition and realizing the hopelessness of battling unarmed, Kness escaped to cover in a nearby ditch.

The gun battle continued as a third CHP cruiser arrived at the scene. More shots were exchanged and both criminals fled in the darkness armed in separate directions. Davis carjacked a parked camper near a dirt road three hours later after a shooting exchange with the owner. He was spotted within hours, pulled over and lacking loaded guns, surrendered.

Three miles away from the parking lot, Twinning broke into a rural house and took the owner hostage. His wife and son escaped and telephoned police who immediately surrounded the house. After hours of negotiation, Twinning released the hostage the next morning. He bragged extensively to his hostage about the previous evenings exploits. As police pumped tear gas into the house and stormed in, Twinning committed suicide with Frago's shotgun.

Davis was sentenced to death for the murders of the four CHP officers. The sentence was commuted to life in prison with the abolishment of the death penalty. He committed suicide while incarcerated at the age of 67 in 2009.

The four slain officers were all between 23-24 years old, married and with a combined total of seven children. Each of them had been with the CHP for less than two years. Post-investigation scrutiny towards the chain of events resulted in approach and training procedural changes as well as upgraded armaments. None of the officers wore bulletproof vests, which might have prevented three of the fatalities.

Today, the stretch of Interstate 5 near the shootings is named after the deceased officers. Signage acknowledging their sacrifice is passed routinely by vacationers visiting the theme park or locals commuting through the now congested Santa Clarita Valley.

As maddeningly stressful and often expensive being pulled over remains to a driver, the inherent risk for each patrolman is significantly steeper.

Newhall CHP Shootout
Restaurant Parking Lot, Henry Mayo Drive Exit

PHOTO:
Site of the parking lot shoot out

Janis Joplin: The Killing Lull Between During A Legendary Recording Session

Three days before her tragic death on October 1, 1970, singer Janis Joplin had completed the track *Mercedes Benz* for her upcoming album *Pearl*, a compilation that would permanently enshrine her fame as a recording artist. The album featured two additional signature works, *Me and Bobby McGee* and *Cry Baby*. Following stints as the lead singer for the groups *Big Brother and the Holding Company* and *Kozmic Blues Band,* she was performing with new accompaniment in the form of the *Full Tilt Boogie Band*.

Completing the final tracks on her new album, the group was preparing for an upcoming fall tour. Joplin was optimistic about her future and particularly pleased by the direction her voice was evolving. While recording in Los Angeles, she and her band stayed at the Landmark Hotel located near the recording studio. The hotel was informally nicknamed the *Land Mine* by guests due to its close proximity to street drug dealers.

Despite her positive perceptions towards her future, Joplin maintained a steady and dangerous dependency on heroin. During the frequent lulls in the recording process, she began dabbling again despite having been reputedly clean for the previous six months.

On the fateful October 4th, Joplin left the recording studio after listening to the band's background tracks for the song *Buried in the Blues*. She intended to return the following day to record her vocal track. Her last sighting was over drinks with band members at local institution *Barney's Beanery*. She reportedly returned to the hotel and shot up with a fix of heroin. She went downstairs and bought a pack of cigarettes in the lobby. She returned back to her room, sat down on the bed and simply fell over before she could light even one. Her head struck the corner of a bedside table causing bleeding on her face. She never regained consciousness.

The heroin was purchased that afternoon from her sole supplier who supposedly was cautious about what he sold. The batch Joplin purchased had not been tested by his normal chemist and was significantly stronger than normal street heroin being 40-50% pure.

The Los Angeles County Coroner ruled her death an *accidental drug overdose.* At the age of twenty-seven, Janis Joplin joined an illustrious group of musicians including Robert Johnson, Jimi Hendrix, Jim Morrison, Brian Jones, Kurt Cobain and Amy Winehouse who would die during that auspicious year of their life.

Former Landmark Motor Hotel
Now Highland Gardens Hotel, Room #105
7047 Franklin Avenue, Hollywood

Pier Angeli: The Burden of Aging in a Youth Driven Business

Approaching 40, actress Pier Angeli concluded that her most desirable acting roles might have already passed her by.

Angeli was born on June 19, 1932 as Anna Maria Pierangeli in Cagliari, Italy. Her twin sister is actress Marisa Pavan. She made her Italian film debut in 1950 in *Tomorrow is Too Late* and launched her American career the following year in *Teresa*. Her film career accelerated rapidly along with the notable men in her life. Kirk Douglas wrote in his autobiography that they became engaged in 1950. She shared a brief romantic relationship with James Dean that ended primarily due to the disapproval of her mother.

In 1954, she married singer and actor Vic Damone. Their divorce four years later ended bitterly with a highly publicized court battle over custody of their son. In 1962, she married Italian composer Armando Trovaji and had another son. During this period, she lived and worked in Italy making periodic films, but her offers for American films evaporated. The couple separated in 1969, but never officially divorced.

Financially destitute following her separation, she returned to Hollywood in 1971 determined to reignite her career. Friends Debbie Reynolds, Agnes Moorehead and her drama coach, Helen Sorell, whom she was living with, assisted her.

Rejection and the torment in waiting for role offers heightened her anxiety. Her final 1971 film appearance in *Octaman* was considered the worst film of her career. The prospect of soon turning forty and the perception that she was no longer employable prompted a desperate response with fatal consequences. On September 10, 1971, she overdosed on barbiturates. She was unaware that she had just received an offer to guest-star in the popular television series *Bonanza*.

Pier Angeli's Suicide Site:
355 South McCarty Drive, Beverly Hills

PHOTO: Helen Sorell's Apartment Complex

Pete Duel: Checking Out At The Crest of Acclaim

One of the most mystifying and unsettling acting deaths was the suicide of Pete Duel on New Years Eve 1971. Born Peter Ellstrom Deuel on February 24, 1940 in Rochester, New York, he was the eldest of three children. His father was a third-generation doctor, but Pete's inclinations drifted towards other interests. After two years of university studies, his father concluded that medicine was not his future and he was squandering his time in school.

His father encouraged Pete to pursue an acting career after viewing him perform in a university production of *The Rose Tattoo*. He soon after landed a role in a New York City touring company. Upon completion, he drove with his mother cross-country in 1963 to pursue his passion and establish his fresh life in Hollywood.

The handsome, clean-cut Duel found minor roles in television work before his casting in the comedy series *Gidget*. After the show's cancellation, he was offered a starring role in the comedy *Love on a Rooftop* that would only last one season. Seeking more serious roles in 1970, he changed the spelling of his name to Duel. He appeared in additional television episodes and feature films before landing his most noteworthy role.

In 1970, Duel became outlaw Hannibal Heyes, alias *Joshua Smith*, appearing opposite Ben Murphy's *Kid Curry* in the television series *Alias Smith and Jones*. The light-hearted Western followed the exploits of two outlaws trying to earn their amnesty. The show became wildly popular and ran 33 episodes accompanied by a television movie with the same name. Following two successful seasons, the show was gearing for its third. Duel had finally discovered a stable and signature part, but apparently not his own fulfillment.

176

Friends and family indicated that he was depressed about a drinking problem that had been accentuated by a DUI incident in June 1971. The accident resulted in injuries to two individuals. The resulting court dates consumed the bulk of his hiatus period between Seasons 1 and 2. He was sentenced to two years probation and required to surrender his driver's license. Through surrounded by a supportive network, Duel expressed exhaustion over his demanding production schedule. His normally placid appearance masked a troubled spirit vainly seeking equilibrium from more than simply public acclaim.

A posthumously published book *Complicated, Simple Me- Peter Deuel: In His Own Words* revealed his thoughts regarding suicide at the age of 16: *There was one thing I didn't have: the guts to take my own life. So, in truth, I just chickened out and after awhile the urge went away.*

It becomes speculative to theorize that Duel eventually found the courage to perform an earlier obsession. It become obvious from reading newspaper and magazine excerpts in the edition that Duel was not as carefree as his on-screen persona, nor simplistic in his expectations towards his life's purpose.

On the evening of December 30, 1971, Duel watched one of his show's episodes with his girlfriend Dianne Ray in his Hollywood Hills home. She fell asleep afterwards in another room while he remained up until midnight. During that period, he abandoned his resolve to quit drinking and drank to excess. Without betraying his motives, Duel entered his bedroom, removed his .38 caliber revolver and said nonchalantly to Ray as he headed towards the living room, *I'll see you later*.

She heard a gunshot and discovered his body lying beneath the Christmas tree. He had placed the pistol to his ear and fired. The bullet tore through his head, shattering a front window and lodged in a carport across the street. He left neither suicide note nor explanation. On January 2, 1972, a memorial service was held at the Self-Realization Fellowship Temple in Pacific Palisades attended by over 1,000 friends and fans. His body was then flown to Penfield, New York for burial.

Following his death, Roger Davis, the show's original narrator, assumed his role. The charismatic Duel proved impossible to replace. The series was cancelled in 1973. Ben Murphy continued a distinguished television and film career over the subsequent three decades, but is still primarily known for his role as *Kid Curry*.

Pete Duel Residence
2552 Glen Green Street, Hollywood

PHOTO: Pete Duel's Former Residence

The Patty Hearst Kidnapping: The Final Nail into the Coffin of Idealism

The kidnapping and subsequent odyssey of Patricia Hearst began on the evening of February 4, 1974. A band of armed men and women knocked on her Berkeley apartment door and within minutes had abducted her, beaten up her fiancé and tossed her into their car truck. They then returned to their headquarters in a Western Addition apartment in San Francisco.

Their 19-year old victim was no average UC Berkeley college student. She was the granddaughter and heiress of publisher William Randolph Hearst.

The kidnapping elevated the status of a group of armed idealists, named the Symbionese Liberation Army (SLA), led by an ex-con named Donald DeFreeze. Hearst's kidnapping was motivated by the group's need to erase the memory of their only known activity up to that time. In November of 1973, the SLA had callously and stupidly murdered Dr. Marcus Foster, the Oakland Superintendent of Schools and seriously wounded his assistant with cyanide-tipped bullets. Two of their shooters were in custody for the murder.

The SLA was an extremist group loaded with guns and rhetoric and an ability to milk media exposure with empty clichéd ideology. Their ranks included both genders, blacks and whites, anarchists and idealists from diverse walks of life.

The SLA had significant propaganda plans for Patty Hearst. After all, what could be more potent to their revolutionary cause than the successful recruitment of an heiress from the elite establishment? Their stated goals included an

180

overthrow of contemporary society.

But first, they had to brainwash and destroy any potential resistance by her. By her account, she was clandestinely housed in a Golden Gate Avenue apartment building in San Francisco. Hearst was blindfolded and isolated in a third floor closet for two months, oblivious to the enormous media frenzy stimulated by her kidnapping. She was repeatedly abused and violated mentally, physically and emotionally. Acceptance and cooperation with their agenda became her sole possibility of survival.

Their brainwashing techniques worked. Hearst was coerced into making inflammatory statements against her family and those she had been closest to before her kidnapping. She integrated seamlessly into SLA operations and ultimately participated in an armed bank robbery in the Sunset district of San Francisco. While captive, the SLA made extravagant ransom requests of her father including demands for distributing millions of dollars in free food to the poor. This audacious stipulation turned into a fiasco with much of the inventory being stolen and disappearing without any form of accountability.

Patty Hearst proved too valuable for the group to release, but their own fate was nearing a violent conclusion. While relatively secure within the Bay Area due to an abundance of safe houses, DeFreeze impulsively opted to shift his operations to Los Angeles. This decision became their undoing.

An unsuccessful petty shoplifting debacle traced the group's van to their temporary residence. The following day on May 17, the Los Angeles police surrounded the house. A massive fuselage followed. Law enforcement officers showed little interest in taking prisoners once they were fired upon. The building went up in flames. Six members of the SLA died in the blaze, including DeFreeze who shot himself fatally while simultaneously on fire.

The site of the destroyed house remained a vacant lot for decades. Today it integrates into the existing neighborhood seemingly buried amidst abundant landscaping foliage

Hearst was not involved in the South Central Los Angeles firefight as she and other members were holed up in an Anaheim hotel room. The remaining SLA gang returned to northern California and disbanded around the country to avoid captures. Hearst was arrested on September 18 and charged with multiple counts including bank robbery.

The judicial circus that followed raised legal liability issues regarding illegal activities performed by forced coercion and brainwashing. Did Hearst fabricate her treatment by the SLA to avoid severe consequences for her actions? There was little doubt that she was unwillingly kidnapped but only Patty Hearst and remaining SLA survivors can attest to the truth towards her subsequent activities and motivations.

The jury at her trial discarded her brainwashing defense. She was found guilty and sentenced to seven years in prison, for which she served two. President Jimmy Carter commuted her sentence and she was later pardoned.

The Heart kidnapping was symptomatic of arguably the most turbulent era of social hostility in San Francisco's history. The abandonment of the peace and love idealism from the prior decade had been eclipsed by a cycle of violence that would haunt the city for the remainder of the decade.

SLA Shootout Location: 1466 East 54th Street Los Angeles.

PHOTO:
Shoot out location in Los Angeles killing six members of the Symbionese Liberation Army.

Golden State Killer: The Triumph of Forensic Evidence

Joseph James DeAngelo was arrested on April 24, 2018 and identified by law enforcement officials as the *Golden State Killer,* also known as the *Original Night Stalker.* Between 1974-1986, 13 murders, 50+ rapes and 120+ burglaries were attributed to this sadistic criminal.

Underexposed by the significant number of serial killers prowling California during the 1970s and overshadowed by the apprehension of one successor Richards Ramirez in 1985, he terrorized both ends of the state with unprecedented horror. The extent of his butchery has never been fully documented.

Most law enforcement observers felt that he might never be apprehended and simply remain as the *one that got away.* In 2016, a renewed effort was initiated to capture the perpetrator. DNA evidence from an earlier Ventura County rape kit attributed to him was entered into a database that identified ten to twenty distant relatives of the killer

A direct linkage was matched to DeAngelo and further implicated him in another unsolved murder attributed to the *Visalia Ransacker.* Between the Spring of 1974 until late 1975, in excess of more than eighty unsolved burglaries plagued Visalia. The serial burglar typically targeted single-family dwellings during late night hours. He would ransacked his target's interiors and generally steal only small insignificant items.

This baffling string of break-ins was climaxed with the invasion of Claude Snelling's home on the late evening of September 11, 1975. Snelling heard an inside disturbance and upon exiting his bedroom discovered a masked intruder attempting to kidnap his daughter. The burglar opened fire on Snelling and fled. Snelling, a journalism professor at the nearby College of the Sequoias died from his wounds.

Three months later police patrols staked out neighborhoods where the intruder had been previously active. A suspect was stopped for questioning. Before his interrogation, he pulled out a handgun and shot at the detective. The bullet shattered the officer's flashlight, but he survived. The shooter escaped into the darkness.

The strange break-ins abruptly ceased in Visalia only to relocate further north within Sacramento and Contra Costa counties. A connection between the two patterns of violence was speculated years later, but never conclusively linked until DeAngelo's capture in 2018.

During his estimated reign of fear, he was suspected to have committed at least fifty sexual assaults. During his northern California rampage, he was labeled the *East Area Rapist*. As his audacity worsened, he was credited with ten confirmed and possibly three additional murders in southern California. DNA matching linked him to the murders.

His confirmed southern California murder victims included Dr. Robert Offerman, Debra Manning, Charlene and Lyman Smith, Keith and Patrice Harrington, Manuela Witthuhn, Cheri Domingo, Gregory Sanchez and Janelle Cruz.

He initially targeted women who were alone in single story residences and then escalated his pattern to couples. He entered the premises during the late night or early morning, awakening his victims. He bound or forced them to bind each other before ruthlessly attacking.

On numerous occasions, a suspect matching his profile was

spotted during neighborhood scouting visits. In one instance a law enforcement officer chased him immediately following a murder and was shot in the head during his pursuit. He survived. From these encounters, a composite drawing and speculative character profile was formulated.

The scariest attribute from his published psychological profile was his ability to blend unnoticeably into mainstream society. His non-threatening appearance, masquerade personality, and cunning made him inconspicuous and dangerous. Little did authorities then realize, he was probably the least conceivable suspect.

Amidst the shadows from which he emerged, the stalker's identity ultimately proved daunting despite his carelessness. He left abandoned weaponry, bicycles and even footprints at murder scenes. His heightened evasion intuition seemed to enable his escapes.

His documented pattern of killings ceased shortly after the mid 1980s. The most common suspicions regarding the *Golden State Killer* were that he may have left California, committed suicide, or even been confined in a mental institution. Several promising suspects had been cleared previously by forensics testing, alibi, or following detailed investigations.

Traditional police methodology would likely have never captured a suspect such as DeAngelo for the simple reason he was a law enforcement officer during the periods when the crimes were committed. He worked three years each in police departments in Exeter (near Visalia) and Auburn (in Sacramento County). In 1979, he was arrested for shoplifting and fired from the Auburn Police force ending his law enforcement career.

Little is known about his background and employment history during the 1980s. In 1980 he purchased a Citrus Heights residence (near Sacramento) where he was ultimately arrested thirty-eight years later. He had been a truck mechanic at a supermarket distribution center between 1990 and his retirement in 2017.

DeAngelo's background does not fit the prototype serial killer profile. He grew up in the Sacramento area, enlisted in the U.S. Navy in 1964 and spent two years during the Vietnam War as a damage controlman on two US carriers. Upon completing his military service, he studied law enforcement and earned a university degree in criminal justice.

His personal life included an estranged marriage and three daughters, two of them born in Sacramento and one in Los Angeles. His impending murder trial will doubtlessly reveal more intimate details about his life and proximity to these crimes when committed. Like the DNA matching profile, his residential and professional history appear to be more than just coincidental.

DeAngelo is currently kept in isolation in the Sacramento County Jail. Six California counties have consolidated their intended prosecution of DeAngelo focusing on 13 counts of murder with special circumstances, 13 counts of kidnapping and a variety of related charges. Most of the rape charges could not be legally pursued due to the state's statute of limitations. The collective counties' strategy is intended to promote a speedier trial and expedient sentencing.

DeAngelo's DNA evidence samples were collected from the door handle of his car and a tissue found in his curbside garbage can. If he is ultimately convicted, this investigative precedent will continue to be actively employed in an attempt to resolve decades of *cold cases* languishing without resolution. For perpetrators who have carelessly left behind evidence in the commission of their crimes, their perception of evading responsibility may eventually become an archaic presumption.

Golden State Killer's Victims:
Professor Claude Snelling: 532 South Whitney, Visalia
Janelle Cruz, 13 Encina, Irvine
Charlene and Lyman Smith: 573 High Point Drive, Ventura
Cheri Domingo and Gregory Sanchez: 449 Toltec Way Golita
Dr. Robert Offerman and Dr. Debra Alexandria Manning: 767 Avenida Pequena, Goleta
Manuela Witthuhn: 35 Columbus, Irvine

PHOTOS:
Claude Snelling's Residence, Janelle Cruz's Residence, Charlene and Lyman Smith's Residence, Cheri Domingo and Gregory Sanchez's Murder Site and Dr. Robert Offerman and Debra Manning's Residence.

Sal Mineo: A Career Comeback Suddenly Curtailed

Sal Mineo's acting career had reached a plateau and decline by the age of 37. He had earned significant praise for his film roles in *Rebel Without A Cause*, *The Man in the Gray Flannel Suit*, *Tonka*, *Exodus* and a variety of television role performances. He had even recorded a record album that featured two top-forty singles.

His exotic appearance and acting skills initially elevated him into matinee idol status with women. His later reputation for homosexuality often precluded his consideration for leading roles. Mineo, like many in his profession was well recognized, but not successful enough to guarantee him prominent career sustainability.

The decline in his public popularity began with his own aging. His most famous roles were based on teenage parts. He acquired enough post-teen acting credits to sustain his credentials, but wealth did not accompany. The apartment complex where he resided was located a block below Hollywood's Sunset Strip, but in a neighborhood that no one would confuse with Beverly Hills.

On February 12, 1976, Mineo was playing the role of a bisexual burglar in a comedy theatre production of *P.S. Your Cat is Dead*. The play had attracted a popular following during its San Francisco run and the cast was preparing for the Los Angeles production.

Arriving at his apartment following a rehearsal, Mineo was approached by Lionel Ray Williams, a pizza deliveryman in a robbery attempt. He was stabbed to death on a spot where his rear driveway intersected with the sloping pathway to his apartment entrance. The knife blade lodged into his heart inducing immediate and fatal internal bleeding. A year after Mineo's death, a similar fatal stabbing occurred in the neighborhood claiming the life of actress Christa Helm. The case remained unsolved until Williams was arrested for the crime.

In 1979, he was tried and convicted for the murder along with ten other robberies in the same area. He was sentenced to 57 years in prison. He was paroled within thirteen years. He would return to familiar incarceration later for assorted crimes. Williams is currently removed from the California prison rolls and presumed living.

Mineo's career may have been resuscitated by his theatre role. The debate is pointless. The entertainment industry habitually has a notoriously short memory span for actors and actresses that have the audacity to age.

Sal Mineo's Apartment Building:
8563 Holloway Drive, West Hollywood

PHOTO: Stabbing occurred in the back alley

Edward Allaway: The Questionable Case For Cured Insanity

Can the criminally insane ever be cured, rehabilitated and released harmlessly back into society?

The question has been elevated into public discussion and policy in the case of Edward Charles Allaway.

On July 12, 1976, Allaway ruthlessly gunned down seven people and wounded two others in the California State University Fullerton library's first floor lobby and basement media center. The dead included Seth Fessenden, Stephen Becker, Paul Herzberg, Bruce Jacobson, Donald Aarges, Frank Teplansky and Deborah Paulsen.

Allaway was a custodian at the library and offered a delusional motive that the victim's were pornographers forcing his estranged wife to appear in their films.

After the shootings, he fled the campus and visited a nearby Anaheim hotel where his separated wife was employed. He telephoned a confession to the police and meekly surrendered.

Years prior to the attack, he had seriously injured a co-worker at a Michigan plant and just before, he had threatened his wife with a knife and subsequently raped her. He had a history of mental illness, which included suicide attempts, institutionalization and electro-shock therapies.

At his trial, he was diagnosed as a paranoid schizophrenic by five different mental health professionals and convicted by a jury on six counts of first-degree murder and one count of second-degree murder. During the sentencing phase of the trial, the jury deadlocked on the state of his mental capacities and the judge ruled him not guilty by reason of insanity. He was committed to the California state mental hospital system commencing at Atascadero State Prison avoiding a prison term. He was subsequently transferred to Napa State Hospital before arriving at his present residence at Patton State Hospital continuing ongoing medical treatment.

No one will ever mistake a mental institution for a maximum-security prison. Inmates have significantly more freedom, space to stroll and direct contact with others including the opposite sex. The law stipulates that convicted defendants found insane must remain institutionalized until they are found sane. The question persists, then what?

In 2009, officials at Patton State Hospital were prepared to release Allaway due to their conclusion that he was no longer suffering from schizophrenia and had been adequately weaned off his medication.

The condition regarding the hospital administrators' own collective sanity and judgment were questioned by then California Attorney General Jerry Brown and Governor Arnold Schwarzenegger. Vehement opposition was voiced by each of the victim's living relatives. They still remain suffering daily from the searing trauma of their loss. The Patton State Hospital administrators withdrew their recommendation for release. In July 2016, he was quietly transferred to Napa State Hospital.

Allaway has on multiple occasions petitioned for his right to be returned back into society.

An imposing question remains as to whether an insane person can be cured? If cured, should he then stand accountable for his heinous actions? Many of the victim's families publicly doubted his insanity claim from the outset. They claimed his violent past was evidence his staged responses were merely a performance.

The ultimate issue however transcends the question of curable mental illness. Is the risk of releasing a mass murderer justifiable to society? Precedent suggests strongly against such a perilous decision.

Edward Allaway Rampage Shooting:
Cal State Fullerton Library Instructional Media Basement, 800 North State College Blvd, Fullerton

PHOTO: Entryway to the new campus library on same site

Roman Polanski: Escaping the Consequences of Rape Using The Genius Defense

In March 1977, film director Roman Polanski, 43, was arrested for his role in a sexual assault of 13-year-old Samantha Jane Gailey. The rape took place at the home of actor Jack Nicholson in the Mulholland Hills of Los Angeles.

Polanski had asked Gailey's mother if he could photograph her daughter as part of an article for the French edition of *Vogue* magazine. Her mother allowed a private shoot that included Polanski request to have Samantha pose topless. He then invited her to a second photo shoot on March 10th at Nicholson's home, who was away on a Colorado ski trip. Samantha reluctantly agreed.

During the course of shooting, Polanski plied her with champagne and they split a Quaalude. Polanski began performing sexual acts upon her despite her protestations. He rationalized in his autobiography that the *sex was consensual* and denied that he drugged her.

Arrested on five counts, Polanski accepted a plea bargain at trial requiring him to plead *guilty* to a lesser charge of *engaging in unlawful sexual intercourse with a minor*. The other four counts were dropped. Under the terms of the plea agreement, the court ordered Polanski to Chino State Prison for a 90-day psychiatric evaluation. He was released after 42 days. His legal team anticipated only a probation term at his subsequent sentencing hearing. His probation officer, the examining psychiatrist and the victim all recommended against incarceration.

The presiding judge at his trial thought otherwise. He suggested to Polanski's attorneys that their client would be sentenced to prison and then deportation. Polanski, skittish to remain and endure prison, purchased a one-way ticket to London and immediately fled. He owned property in England, but understanding the extradition policies of the United Kingdom, continued on to France where he was a dual citizen along with his native Poland.

Since his 1977 flight, Polanski has avoided traveling and working in countries with readily enforced American extradition treaties. He was detained at the Zurich Airport during September 2009 while attending the Zurich Film Festival honoring him with a lifetime achievement award. For nine months, he was held in detention while a Swiss Federal Criminal Court and then Supreme Court reviewed the US Department of Justice request for extradition. In July 2010, the Swiss court rejected the American request and Polanski was released.

The decision proved controversial internationally. The foreign ministers of France and Poland initially urged Switzerland to release Polanski but subsequently withdrew their support for him. The base of his support has always stressed his contributions to the film industry, but generally has remained mute regarding the severity of his crime.

A truism regarding the American criminal justice system has always existed that the worst trait a suspected perpetrator can possess is poverty. The hypocrisy surrounding a talented filmmaker and his criminal act may possibly never find conventional resolution within his lifetime. He will remain free from incarceration unless his cautionary prudence again takes a false and impulsive step towards the allure of recognition.

Roman Polanski Rape Site
12850 Mulholland Drive, Beverly Hills

PHOTO: Entrance to the rape location

The Hillside Strangler Duo: Killing Cousins

The Hillside Strangler tandem of Kenneth Bianchi and Angelo Buono paralyzed Los Angeles and particularly the San Fernando Valley during four months between November 1977 and February 1978. Ten young women were kidnapped, raped, tortured and then killed. Their bodies were randomly dumped in locations ranging from the Forest Lawn Cemetery to residential driveways. The empty hillside dumping terrains earned them their designation.

Bianchi and Buono were cousins bonded in decadence. Initial investigations focused on the responsible party being a single individual. The evidence and patterns of torture revealed the characteristics of a lethal duo.

There were no survivors from their attacks. The confirmed dead included Yolanda Washington, Judith Miller, Lissa Kastin, Dolores Cepeda, Sonja Johnson, Kristina Weckler, Jane King (the oldest victim at 28), Lauren Wagner, Kimberly Martin and Cindy Hudspeth. Others victims likely existed but escaped attribution to the murderers.

One potential victim was reportedly spared. The killers gave a ride to Catharine Lorre, the daughter of actor Peter Lorre with the intent of killing her. Once they determined her identity, they released her without incident. Were they paying homage to his work as a screen killer? More likely they preferred to keep their killings spree under the international publicity radar.

The heat of intensive investigation separated the two cousins. Bianchi fled to Bellingham, Washington where his personal rampage continued with a rape and murder of two women, Karen Mandic and Diane Wilder, he had lured into a home for a housesitting position. He was arrested soon afterwards.

Buono remained in Glendale where he operated an auto body repair business on prominent Colorado Boulevard. His business location was situated centrally to the killings. He was arrested without incident.

Bianchi attempted a poorly executed insanity defense at his trial. A court appointed psychologist conclusively observed that he was faking. Both men were convicted to life sentences since the death penalty had been abolished in California. Buono died of a heart attack in 2002 while incarcerated and Bianchi remains imprisoned at the Washington State Penitentiary in Walla Walla for murders in that state.

Angelo Buono's Former Auto Upholster Shop Location: 703 East Colorado Street, Glendale.

Freddie Prinze: The Evening The Comic Became Humanized and the Laughter Abruptly Ceased

By the age of 22, Freddie Prinze had achieved superstardom with his role as *Chico* in the television series *Chico and the Man.* Starring opposite crusty Jack Albertson, the show provided Prinze with an ideal outlet for his improvisational humor, skills honed from working the comedy club circuit in New York City.

Suited for the role of class clown, Prinze had his first national exposure on one of the last episodes of *Jack Paar Tonite.* Expanded limelight followed with appearances on *The Tonight Show Starring Johnny Carson,* which he guest hosted on several occasions while Carson was vacationing. The public's insatiable demand for his humor made him a frequent guest at celebrity roasts and on variety shows. In 1976, he signed a lucrative five-year contract with NBC.

As his professional life accelerated, his personal life disintegrated. In October 1975, he married Katherine Cochran. They had one son together who would become future actor Freddie Prinze Jr. Fame and massive fan adoration unhinged their union. On November 16, 1976, Prinze was arrested for driving under the influence of Quaaludes. A few weeks later, his wife filed for divorce.

His depression worsened in the weeks following the filing. On the evening of January 28, 1977, he spoke with his estranged wife from the Beverly Hills Plaza Hotel where he had been residing since their separation. That evening, he reportedly made numerous farewell calls to family members and friends and also penned a suicide note. He received a visit from his business manager and with him looking on put a gun to his head and pulled the trigger.

Prinze reportedly had a macabre fascination with Russian roulette that often frightened his friends. If this indeed was his intent, he lost the gamble. The shot did not kill him instantly and he was placed on life support following emergency surgery at the UCLA Medical Center. His family removed him from the life sustaining equipment the following day and he died at approximately 1:00 p.m.

His suicide abruptly ceased the perception of a carefree personality enjoying the benefits of a sprinters pace to fame. His career ended so fleetingly it never even had time to suffer a lull.

Freddy Prinze's Suicide Location:
Beverly Hills Plaza Hotel, Room 216
10300 Wilshire Boulevard, Los Angeles

PHOTO: Beverly Hills Plaza Hotel

The Contract Killing of Vic Weiss: The Payback For Stealing

The double existence of Vic Weiss culminated in the closely confined trunk of his luxurious red and white Rolls Royce.

Weiss impersonated business prowess and the epitome of skilled achievement. His acquaintance base included high-level athletic personalities. He postured in designer suits, a gold Rolex watch and prominent diamond ring. Most of his friends and acquaintances assumed he had acquired his fortune through real estate, insurance ventures and ownership stakes in a Ford and Rolls Royce dealerships in Van Nuys. Weiss had a reputation for always paying any entertainment tab involving his friends and business associates.

In 1979, his highest profile friend was University of Nevada Las Vegas (UNLV) Basketball Coach Jerry Tarkanian, a Pasadena high school classmate. Their formative bond and mutual respect were sustained over the ensuing years as Weiss began to dabble professionally in sport management. Tarkanian become one of his early clients and Weiss was in the midst of negotiating a prestigious contract on his behalf.

Real Estate developer Jerry Buss was in the final stages of purchasing the Los Angeles Lakers from Jack Kent Cooke and wanted a renowned winning coach to lead the Lakers. He desired the services of Tarkanian whose reputation for winning and feuding with the NCAA were legendary. The NCAA (National College Athletic Association) is the organizing authority, which legislates and governs amateur athletics within the American university sports system.

203

On the afternoon of June 14, 1979, Cooke, Buss and Weiss met at the Beverly Comstock Hotel to negotiate and finalize verbal agreements for Tarkanian's services. The session ended positively. The concurring terms were handwritten on a piece of paper and dropped into Weiss' briefcase upon the session's conclusion.

Official notification and consent by Tarkanian and a signed printed contract were the sole obstacles to a finalized agreement.

Weiss was supposed to telephone Tarkanian with the encouraging news. Afterwards he was scheduled to dine at a San Fernando Valley restaurant with his wife. Neither the anticipated call nor the dinner materialized.

Weiss disappeared. Four days later a security guard at the Universal Sheraton Hotel parking garage spotted his Rolls Royce with the stunning gold interior and putrid odor. Investigators found Weiss' decomposed remains shoved into the trunk. Robbery did not appear to be the motive. He was still wearing his diamond ring and Rolex. His briefcase was conspicuously absent. He had been efficiently executed by two gunshots into the back of his head.

His illusionary posed lifestyle and a motive eventually became exposed.

He was not wealthy. His business ventures and car dealerships proved fictitious. His Rolls Royce was leased. Emerging details clarified his actual occupation as an organized crime money launderer. He was in significant debt due to gambling losses. To substantiate his image, rumors circulated that he may have siphoned funds from his employers.

The code of conduct demanded by the criminal class is absolute fidelity and ethics. Non-compliance or violation is punished by immediate disposability. Weiss pilfered from the wrong source and his compensation became academic.

To reinforce discipline, silence becomes paramount, particularly with law enforcement authorities. The investigation into Weiss' death led only to additional suspicious deaths of related parties with no conclusive answers or cooperation. Investigators concluded that Weiss' killing was a professional contract hit. No one has ever been arrested for the crime.

The Los Angeles Lakers did not hire Jerry Tarkanian. The exemplary playing talents of Ervin Magic Johnson and the coaching by three relative unknowns, elevated the team into one of elite sports franchises of the 1980s. Tarkanian remained at UNLV until 1992, peaking his stint with a title at the NCAA Championship in 1990. Two years later, he accepted a head-coaching job with the San Antonio Spurs professional basketball club. He was unceremoniously fired after a single season. He returned to college basketball and authority defiance at Fresno State University between 1995-2002. He retired with an enviable head coaching record of 706 wins and 198 losses. He died in February 2015.

His success, strategy tactics and accompanying controversy altered a perception of amateurism within college basketball. His vehement supporters argued that he accomplished incredible results with inferior talent. His critics claimed his flagrant recruitment violations often involved unscrupulous financial offers.

The divisions between professionalism and amateur athletics continue to blur. Winning college athletic programs with their accompanying financial benefits remain the justifiable motives for stretching ethical boundaries. Within professional athletics, gambling interests have always tested the legitimacy of outcomes. The scale and infusions of betting that taint performances are revealed periodically. Only inside manipulators know the extent of how rampant the disease affects sporting competitions globally.

The example of Vic Weiss' killing had absolutely no adverse impact on the expansion of sports wagering. Global betting has since proliferated multifold. Internet sports sites, fantasy fan programs and television programming relentlessly fuel spectator's insatiable demand.

Individual performance, team examinations and highlight filming are marketed ceaselessly as viewing spectacles. Professional athletics has elevated itself into an international and cultural obsession diverting attention from more immediate, substantive and profound social and political issues.

Vic Weiss became a casualty of his gambling compulsion. His excesses are hardly unique. At some juncture, contemporary society will be obliged to reconcile the damage, blindness and sickness imposed by our healthy obsession with organized sporting competitions.

Vic Weiss Body Discovered:
Sheraton Universal Parking Garage, 333 Universal
Hollywood Drive, Universal City

PHOTO:
Parking garage at the Universal Sheraton Hotel

Raymond Washington: A Cycle of Senseless Violence Devours A Former Founder

It was fatalistic that the patriarch who elevated Los Angeles gang warfare should be eliminated by one of his descendants.

On August 10, 1979 at approximately 10 p.m., 25-year-old Raymond Washington was gunned down on the corner of South San Pedro and 64th Street in the South Central district of Los Angeles. He was the victim of yet another drive-by shooting. He appeared familiar with his killers. A passenger leveled him fatally with a sawed-off shotgun as he approached their vehicle. He died two hours later. There was no clear motive, no suspects and once again, no coherence behind the slaying.

Washington's notoriety was based on being a founding member of the violent African-American Crips street gang recruited from the housing projects of Watts. Their lethal feuds with another gang, the Bloods from Compton and other affiliated gangs became legendary urban lore. Their rivalry was visually differentiated by distinctive apparel colors, graffiti symbolism and hand gestures.

A disintegrating cycle of violence and death encircled Washington's brief life ultimately strangling him. He was the youngest son of four from a broken home. He spent the second half of the 1970s in prison and detachedly observed a transformation in the scope of gang operations. Neighborhood gangs were initially organized under the guise of neighborhood protection and security. Their orientation changed.

Washington's forte was his intimidating muscular physique, meanness and proficiency in fistfights. During his

208

incarceration, the rival conflicts escalated into weaponry. By the time of his release, Washington had no more control over the gang he founded than keeping the violence contained. Lucrative drug distribution and extortion had altered the financial orientation of gangs and infighting became inherent between competitors.

Washington's prison stay had effectively relinquished any control he might have once commanded. Aside from his expressed interest in consolidating the various regional gangs into a united organization, he was adamantly opposed to infringing immigration into his controlled neighborhood environment. Organized street gang membership and illicit activity has since spread internationally.

A life constructed on blood feuds typically can have only a singular outcome. There are no memorials commemorating Raymond Washington's life within his neighborhood or death site. Instead, graffiti, discarded furniture and a pronounced absence of urban Los Angeles economic vitality remain.

A variety of diverse ethnicities have since infiltrated South Central Los Angeles necessitated by economics. The poor and disenfranchised are obliged to pay cheaper rents with compromised security. The terrain is terrifying to outsiders and an incentive for the ambitious raised there to vacate when circumstances allow.

Could Raymond Washington's life been redeemed or transformed? Two of his top associates, Stanley *Tookie* Williams and Gregory *Batman* Davis initiated efforts via children's books and non-profit organizations to combat movements they helped pioneer. Williams' was executed at San Quentin in 2005 for killing four individuals in two separate armed robberies.

Any moral behind his death has been obscured behind the grim statistics of subsequent senseless fatalities. Lifestyle glorifications through popular films, music and clothing trends have created a gang fashion chic. The horrifying realities reveal a more severe and sobering scenario.

Buoyancy is a fragile commodity for the young men and women of South Central Los Angeles. Their odds of violent death multiply the longer they reside on their vicious streets and choose to participate in an affiliate gang.

Raymond Washington helped create the monster that ultimately devoured him. Other ambitious successors wait their turn.

Raymond Washington's Shooting Site:
Corner of Sixty-fourth and San Pedro Street, Los Angeles

The Unfulfilled Crossover of Dorothy Stratten

Unrealized potential is a curse that has haunted emerging talents seemingly forever in disciplines as diverse as the performing arts, politics, sports and business. The space for the upper echelon of achievement is precariously limited. Timing, persistence and opportunity are often more crucial than raw talent.

Through no fault of her own, Dorothy Ruth Stratten (born Hoogstraten) was denied her aspirations to entertainment stardom following a promising beginning.

Emerging from suburban Coquitlam, adjacent to Vancouver, Stratten met Paul Snider, a local nightclub and promoter of diversely unsuccessful schemes at seventeen while working at a local *Dairy Queen*. Snider, nine years her senior, seduced the impressionable and physically stunning blond and blue-eyed Stratten. During the summer of 1978, with her mother's consent, he had professional nude photographs taken of her. He mailed the photographs to the editorial offices of *Playboy* magazine and interest was immediate.

Dorothy Stratten relocated to Los Angeles and ascended quickly within the *Playboy* hierarchy. She found employment as a bunny waitress at their Century City Nightclub and was selected as the August 1979 *Playmate of the Month*. 1980 *Playmate of the Year* honors soon followed. Her meteoric rise was gradually severing Snider's control despite his having coerced her into a marriage ceremony in June of 1979 in Las Vegas.

Snider had outgrown his usefulness and was universally perceived by her surrounding support team as a parasitic presence exhibiting erratic and overly possessive behavior.

Stratten supported Snider financially throughout their marriage due to his inability to work legally with his Canadian nationality and his lack of a work visa. Her expanding prospects enabled no place for a limited capacity hustler. Snider had no intention of allowing his protégé to elude his stifling and desperate grasp.

Stratten was channeling her energies professionally and in her personal life elsewhere. Between 1979-80, she appeared in the light comedy films *Americathon*, *Skatetown USA*, *Autumn Born* and *Galaxina*, plus television episodes of *Buck Rogers in the 25th Century* and *Fantasy Island*. She was cast for a prominent role in Peter Bogdanovich's directed *They All Laughed*, a film that would be released in late 1980 following her death.

While none of these works remotely teased Oscar nominations, she had demonstrated crossover talent potential, unique within the Playmate selection universe. Her personal appeal, ambition and drive were encouraging signs. Her entertainment industry contact base was elevating. She had begun an affair with Bogdanovich during filming. He had similarly mentored actress Cybill Shepherd in the earliest stages of her career. Stratten moved in with him and officially separated from Snider.

Paul Snider coaxed her into one final visit at their former West Hollywood apartment during the daylight hours of August 14, 1980. Their discussion was intended towards arranging terms for a divorce agreement. Snider was sharing the residence with the building's owner. Other guests were present that day but allowed the couple their privacy.

Upon arrival, Snider escorted her into their former bedroom and closed the door. He immediately bound her without

213

creating a disturbance or outburst and sexually assaulted her. He then blasted her with a shotgun he had recently acquired and turned the weapon on himself to complete the murder-suicide. Their strewn bodies were discovered without clothing several hours later. No one had overheard the commotion. Dorothy Stratten was 20 years and her potential and mainstream exposure was terminated.

Her brief life and tragic death prompted two exploitive films *Death of a Centerfold* and *Star80* (her personalized car license plate), several books and even musical recordings. Bogdanovich, in perhaps the oddest follow-up twist, financed her younger sister Louise's education and modeling classes following her death. He then married her at 20, the identical age he had lost Dorothy. The union lasted 13 years before a divorce in 2001. His gesture bore an ironical resemblance to Orpheus attempting to retrieve and reconstruct his beloved wife Eurydice from death and the underworld.

Dorothy Stratten was supplanted in 1981 as the annually honored Playmate by another striking beauty. Playboy Enterprises today lingers on the periphery of the cultural relevance it once commanded. The organization has lost the majority of its following and influence due to an aging readership and more explicit Internet viewing outlets. None of Stratten's successors have successfully bridged the transition from nude modeling into major entertainment success.

Dorothy Stratten Murder:
10881 Clarkson Road, Los Angeles

PHOTO:
Apartment murder site

Darby Crash: The Germ Who Left Little Trace

The Germs represented the crash and burn destructive philosophy underlying punk rock. The combative and chaotic theatrics of their live performances gashed a protruding artery of profanity and violence onto its diminutive audiences. The band would be banned from nearly every Los Angeles rock club, but periodically played as *Alias G. I.*, initials for *Germs Incognito*.

Lead singer Darby Crash's brief life began unruly and ended abruptly. Aside from his over-the-top staged performance in the punk rock documentary *The Decline of Western Civilization*, his and *The Germs* impact within the music industry was minimal. One group member, who never played a live set due to an extended bout of mononucleosis, was drummer Belinda Carlisle. She would later flourish as the lead singer for *The Go-Go's*.

Darby Crash was born as Jan Paul Beahm in Baldwin Hills Hospital and raised in Culver City. At the age of 11, his eldest brother (27) died of a heroin overdose. He never knew his father who was reportedly a Swedish sailor and lived the majority of his life with his mother, who suffered from mental illness resulting in erratic and abusive behavior.

Crash attended an alternative high school in West Hollywood where the students were allowed to create their own curriculum. He was dismissed in 1976 for subversive behavior that he blamed on his frequent LSD use.

The Germs were an incarnation from several previous bands. The interaction between performers and audience was usually hostile. The Los Angeles Police Department frequently intervened forcing the band to end their performances prematurely. Their last official show before disbanding was performed in April 1980 at the Fleetwood in Redondo Beach. The group reunited for a reunion performance on December 3rd at the *Starwood Nightclub* in West Hollywood. Crash used the money from the reunion show to purchase a lethal dose of heroin for two.

Four days later, Crash entered into a suicide pact with female friend and Germs drummer Casey Cola Hopkins. They chose a converted garage at her mother's house to shoot up. He injected Casey first and them himself. She survived to recount the story. He didn't.

An imaginative tale emerged that he attempted to scrawl *Here Lies Darby Crash* on the wall as he was expiring. In reality, he left only a handwritten note written before he injected both of them leaving his few possessions to the group's bass player.

Darby Crash and *The Germs* have been profiled periodically since his death. The timing of his suicide proved problematic for any significant media attention. The day following, Mark David Chapman shot Beatle John Lennon fatally in the archway of his residence, *The Dakota*, in New York City.

Darby Crash's Suicide Location
137 North Fuller Avenue, Los Angeles

PHOTO: Darby Crash's Suicide Site

The Wonderland Gang Killings and Fantasy Sex Industry

Pornography legend John Holmes lived a multiple existence. While considered an industry icon due to the size of his penis and acting appearances in over 2,500 films, Holmes was a notorious drug addict.

His addiction ingratiated him into distribution rings including organized crime figure and nightclub owner Eddie Nash and the Wonderland Gang, based in a wooded Laurel Canyon neighborhood in the San Fernando Valley.

These ruthless acquaintances culminated in disaster when Holmes skimmed currency and drugs from the Wonderland gang to support his own habit. Holmes tipped his debtors off about an extensive stash of drugs, money and jewelry Nash had stored in his residence. On June 29, 1981, the gang broke into Eddie Nash's opulent home and staged a large-scale armed robbery.

Robbing a competitor is always a poor idea. Retribution was swift and within two days. Holmes, whose acting range withered in proportion to his most marketable asset, was unable to mask his participation. Nash forcibly coerced his confession and obliged Holmes to accompany a revenging group under his hire.

Nash ruthlessly avenged the theft. During the early hours of July 1, the Laurel Canyon drug headquarters were invaded. Five of the members were attacked and four died from extensive blunt force trauma injuries from hammers and pipes.

The dead included leader Billy DeVerell, Ron Launius, Joy Miller and Barbara Richardson. Launius's wife, Susan

Launius, miraculously survived the attack but had to have part of her skull surgically removed. These casualties were not innocent victims. The crime scene and the carnage were brutal and excessive. John Holmes was a spectator to insure his silence.

Nash, his bodyguard Gregory Diles and Holmes were arrested, tried and acquitted for the murders. Holmes refused to testify or cooperate for obvious reasons. His participation would have insured his death upon release. He remained in jail for several months adamant in his refusal and noncompliance. Diles died in 1995 and Nash in 2014.

In 1998, Holmes died of complications as a result of AIDS. An accumulated lifestyle of promiscuous sex with both genders fueled by intravenous drug use ultimately caught up with him. Even on his deathbed, he refused to cooperate with law enforcement authorities.

The Wonderland Gang murders remain officially unsolved. They were loosely depicted in the successful film *Boogie Nights*. Despite Holmes' ability to earn premium wages for film appearances, he died destitute in a VA Medical Center in Los Angeles. The majority of his earnings lined his nasal passages via an unconquerable cocaine habit.

Holmes is still regarded as the most renowned male pornography actor of all time. The price and value for this fame was devalued by his pathetic addictions, betrayals and their accompanying consequences.

Wonderland Murders:
8763 Wonderland Avenue, Studio City

PHOTO:
Site of the killing

John Belushi: The Train Collision No One Could Slow Down

Few people were surprised that comedian John Belushi nourished a destructive drug habit. He parodied his own excesses with his comic material. His renowned manic energy and documented appetite devoured food, alcohol and controlled substances with the same ferocity as a gambler parlaying a winning streak.

At 33, he was in the midst of a professional losing streak. His hedonistic habits had shoved his health onto a desperate precipice. His 1981 films *Continental Divide* and *Neighbors* fared dismally at the box office and his most notable works with *Saturday Night Live* and *Animal House* were a distant memory from three and four years before. *The Blues Brothers* film in the early 80s had cultivated a cult following, but financially never compensated for the hyperinflated budget.

There were film and television projects pending, but the greatest concern became whether Belushi could remain sober and healthy enough to complete them.

On February 28, 1982, Belushi checked into the Chateau Marmont Hotel where he had reserved his favorite bungalow. He had lodged previously at the property and found their accommodating and discreet services ideal for his preference to remain incognito.

Within his expensive bungalow, Belushi lived in an accumulating squalor. The interior was trashed and littered with discarded food containers, wine bottles and dirty laundry. His shambled existence represented the ultimate catastrophe Belushi was courting. The room was stocked with an unlimited stream of cocaine and a companion enabler named Cathy Smith who facilitated Belushi's desire to inject heroin, whenever desired.

Belushi's intentions for his West Coast residence was to focus on drafting a comedy script for a film titled *Noble Rot*. The plot centered on a robbery scheme set amidst the early California wine industry. The project was proceeding abysmally and suitor Paramount Pictures was dissatisfied with the progress. His previous credentials kept the thin communication lines active.

Belushi's appearance and personality were reportedly floundering and his drug addiction worsened the prognosis. His attention span became scattered, conversation incoherent and his appearance unkempt. Observers noted that he didn't appear to be bathing or shaving regularly and was barely sleeping. He missed or was frequently late to scheduled meetings and appointments. His erratic behavior became disconcerting, but who was in a position to slow John Belushi from his own self-destructiveness?

On Thursday evening, March 4th, actors Robert De Niro and Harry Dean Stanton attempted to coax Belushi into joining them on their evening escapades. They and later comedian Robin Williams ultimately visited his bungalow but didn't remain long. The threesome proved useless in offering any tangible assistance. DeNiro and Williams reportedly did indulge in some of his cocaine piled on the dining room table. The last visitor exited at approximately 3 a.m.

Around noon the following day, Belushi was discovered unconscious by his personal trainer and bodyguard, Bill Wallace. Cathy Smith had vacated the bungalow earlier that morning. By her account, he was still alive and snoring loudly. What she attempted to suppress was that she had injected him with a fatal combination of heroin and cocaine.

Wallace attempted CPR in vain. When the ambulance arrived, the medical team did not attempt to resuscitate Belushi. The needle tracks on his arms clearly indicated a drug overdose and Belushi had already expired.

The unfinished business that remained was a rationale behind those closest to him as to why intervention became impossible to prevent the inevitable. Belushi clearly wasn't ready for their help nor did he expressively desire anyone's assistance. It is equally the privilege and tragedy of fame. In 1984, author Bob Woodward published a painstakingly researched and scathing biography about Belushi's decline, final days and hours. Two years later, Cathy Smith pleaded no contest to *involuntary manslaughter* for injecting him with his final destructive dose.

Behind their exuberant appearance, many comedians overcompensate their desperate anxieties with excess. Fifteen years later, another *Saturday Night Live* cast member Chris Farley would overdose from a combination of cocaine and morphine at the identical age as Belushi. Robin Williams would hang himself in 2014 and numerous other comic performers have died prematurely. Their paths of self-destruction are littered with furtively motivated assistance. Belushi, Farley and Williams' comic material remain hilarious even today, but in hindsight, did each really enjoy the bullet ride to the top?

John Belushi Overdose Location:
Chateau Marmont Hotel, Bungalow 3
8221 Sunset Boulevard, Hollywood

PHOTOS: Chateau Marmont Hotel

The Consequences of Poorly Administrated Justice and Subsequent Karma

Dominique Dunne was born into an arts industry family with father Dominick Dunne a writer, producer, and actor. One of her older brothers, Griffin Dunne is an actor and she was the niece of married novelist John Gregory Dunne and Joan Didion. Her formative studies were acting oriented and at the age of twenty, earned her first television and film roles. In 1981, she was cast in her initial feature film *Poltergeist* and was accumulating an impressive body of work.

In 1981, she met John Thomas Sweeney, a sous-chef at the prestigious *Ma Maison* restaurant at a party. Following a few weeks of dating, they impulsively moved in together into a one-bedroom West Hollywood house. The decision was tainted from the outset due to Sweeney's jealousy and possessiveness.

The couple fought often and violently. Sweeney reportedly yanked clumps of hair from her scalp during one encounter and beat her frequently. He once tried to strangle her. She returned to the abuse, but in September 1982, finally broke off the relationship. When he moved out, she changed the locks, but couldn't alter his obsession.

One month later while she was rehearsing for a miniseries role with a fellow actor, Sweeney telephoned and then showed up at her residence. She reluctantly agreed to speak to him through a locked rear door before consenting to talk with him directly on the front porch.

An argument ensued escalating into violence with Sweeney striking Dunne and then viciously strangling her for three minutes on the driveway. She was transferred to Cedars-

Sinai Medical Center where she remained on life support for five days, dying the same day that her parents authorized her removal.

Sweeney was originally charged with attempted murder. That was modified to first-degree murder upon her death. Sweeney readily confessed to killing Dunne adding pathetically that he had tired to kill himself as well. No evidence corroborated his claim towards attempted suicide.

The controversial trial of Sweeney witnessed one of the worst travesties in sentencing conceivable. The presiding judge Burton S. Katz suppressed testimony from a key prosecution witness, a former girlfriend of Sweeney's who'd detailed his violent past with her. The judge also ruled that the evidence allowed and presented was insufficient to convict Sweeney of first-degree murder since in his opinion no evidence of predetermination or deliberation was evident. He instructed the jury that they were only allowed to consider charges of manslaughter or second-degree murder.

After eight days of deliberation, the jury acquitted Sweeney of second-degree murder and found him guilty of voluntary manslaughter. Judge Katz criticized the jury for their decision, but he received the harshest criticism for his suppression of evidence. Sweeney received a sentence of six years in prison, the maximum possible, but served only three years and eight months.

Bad karma historically has serious consequences.

The presiding judge Katz was transferred to the Juvenile Court system in Sylmar shortly after the trial. He retired unceremoniously and authored a book in 2009 entitled *Justice Overruled: Unmasking the Criminal Justice System.*

His intent was to expose the abuses of the justice system and what could be done to fix it. In the minds of many John Sweeney trial observers, a mirror might have better served as the most accurate form of assessment.

John Sweeney found employment as the head chef at an upscale Santa Monica restaurant only three months after his prison release. Dunne family members handed out protest fliers to restaurant patrons forcing Sweeney to quit and relocate. Dominick Dunne hired a private investigator to track Sweeney's movements and actions. His trail continued to Florida and then to the Pacific Northwest where he changed his name to John Maura. Shortly before his death from bladder cancer in 2009, Dominick Dunne ceased the pursuit. Sweeny (now Maura) reportedly became the General Manager of Food Services for retirement home complex in San Rafael, California.

His evasion of an appropriate prison sentence for his callous murder will likely trail him as bloody footprints throughout the remainder of his life.

Dominique Dunne's Residence
8723 Rangely Avenue, West Hollywood

PHOTO: Murder site

Dennis Wilson Drowning: The First To Descend Permanently

Dennis Wilson was the sole Beach Boy that could actually surf. He was also the first member of the band to die tragically. For all of the sunshine melodic harmonies the band has radiated for nearly six decades, a darkened legacy has tainted the Wilson family. Most observers concluded the first band member to exit prematurely would have been Brian Wilson. He miraculously survived his own willing plunges into self-destruction.

Dennis was the original drummer, but was estranged for periods of time from the band and replaced in the recording sessions. He was considered the best looking member and parlayed the group's success into gluttonous spending, drug addiction, chasing sex and developing odd liaisons. He invited Charles Manson and his *family* into his Sunset Boulevard home participating in their orgies and other debauchery.

He married five times including the illegitimate daughter of his cousin and fellow band member Mike Love. He fathered four documented children. His excesses led him into the inevitable train wreck those closest to him anticipated.

He would not reach the age of forty or 1984. On Christmas day, 1983 he picked a fight with a male friend of his latest estranged wife at the Santa Monica Bay Inn. The same morning, he had checked himself out of the detoxification unit at St. John's Hospital and Health Center locally. He began drinking immediately afterwards before instigating the fight. He was beaten badly necessitating another return to the hospital.

The detox unit declined to accept him back and he was obliged to check into Daniel Freeman Marina Hospital at around 2 a.m. where he spent the night.

Three days later, his body was pulled out of the murky waters of Marina Del Rey following a drinking binge on a friend's boat in one of the Marina's slips. While on board, he developed an abrupt compulsion to go diving for *treasures* underwater in the 58-degree waters. Toxicology tests indicated that his blood alcohol level exceeded twice the legal limit for driving.

He made his final dive and was viewed rising approximately two feet from the surface. He never surfaced. His boating companions became worried. The harbor patrol searched the waters for approximately thirty minutes before finding his body. He was pronounced dead immediately.

The Beach Boys resumed performing approximately one month following his death. They have toured perpetually to maintain their extravagant lifestyles threatened by prior financial mismanagement. Their recordings and fresh material has never regained the commercial acclaim of their early records.

They sing to legions of loyal fans reminiscing about dreamy summers past, drag racing and social rivalries. As the original members all exceed seventy, the spectacle borders as a cross between irony and comedy.

Dennis Wilson's Accidental Death Site
Basin C-1100, Marina Del Rey

PHOTOS: Basin C Boat Slip

Marvin Gaye: A Visionary Dishonored Within His Household

Singer Marvin Gaye understood the capricious world of music industry popularity. His sheer talent and stage charisma had vaulted him into international stardom. A mid-career lapse, accentuated by family and personal demons had once consigned him into tax exile and potentially career oblivion. At the peak of an improbable comeback, the man responsible for his birth felled him cruelly.

During 1978, amidst a career crater, he had divorced his wife Anna Gordy, the sister of Motown Record owner Barry Gordy. Motown was Gaye's record label and tantamount to his early success. As a partial payment towards her alimony settlement, Gaye recorded a bitter divorce tirade of an album *Here, My Dear*. The album was a commercial failure. Gaye vanished into a professional hiatus.

Scaling rapid unimaginable heights only to plunge into their accompanying precipices became a familiar pattern for Gaye. The relationship with his minister father, Marvin Gay, Sr. endured similar extremes. As Pentecostal performers, their accompaniments were brilliant. Offstage during his teenage years, Gaye, Jr. was disciplined often and frequently kicked out of his father's house. He discontinued his high school studies and enlisted in the Air Force. He was later discharged for insubordination.

Marvin Jr. was restless but musically brilliant.

Following his return to hometown Washington D.C., he performed with touring vocal groups. His growing reputation expanded his exposure as a desirable background session singer for established music acts. These assignments attracted the attention of Barry Gordy and his fledging Motown Records.

Under Gordy's tutelage and Motown's rise, his career, stage presence and songwriting capabilities flourished. His diversified skills earned him paid assignments to play drums in recording sessions and with touring groups.

The emotional rift with his father did not entirely heal with time and distance. He added an "e" to his surname to distance himself from his father's influence and the accompanying homosexual slang references. As international tastes discovered the Motown sound, Gaye prospered as one of its most marketable acts. His career and exposure skyrocketed.

He teamed with singer Tammi Terrell on successful duets. She collapsed in his arms during a 1967 performance and was diagnosed with a malignant brain tumor. Her career was finished. She died three years later from brain cancer.

Gaye's trajectory accelerated. His simplistic love ballad recordings during the late 1960s were surpassed by his finest work in 1971. He released his classic *What's Going On*. The album featured the probing depth and timeless societal questioning. The theme was inspired by Gaye's insightful and stark observations of police brutality during anti-war rallies in Berkeley.

The masterpiece severed an introspective nerve in the listening public elevating previously catchy love compositions into a more sustained and complicated pleas towards social consciousness. His lyrics still achingly resonate and reverberate with truth. The lyrics uniquely crossed color lines and illuminated society's sense of estrangement and desperation. The timely songs issued a call towards collective action and healing that remains mute to much of society.

He followed up this commercial breakthrough with the albums *Let's Get It On* and a motion picture soundtrack for the film *Trouble Man*. He began touring internationally and receiving his due acclaim as a substantive voice. His live concert album sales substantiated his stellar performance credentials.

At the absolute pinnacle of commercial success, the adulation and praise shifted. His contentious divorce, rampant cocaine use and a shift in popular music towards disco, temporarily made his own works too sobering for public consumption. His attempts to replicate the senseless dance rhythms of a trending fad proved futile. Marvin Gaye, like so many of his soul music peers, could not evolve in reverse gear. By the conclusion of the decade, social consciousness was no longer in vogue and rampant consumerism was the replacing deity.

Gaye relocated to London to avoid potential imprisonment for back taxes exceeding $4.5 million. His cocaine dependency worsened and his life spiraled into freefall.

Amidst a wreckage of despair and self-loathing, he returned to his elemental strengths. In 1981, he relocated to Ostend, Belgium and began recording new compositions. He curtailed his drug use, began exercising rigorously and performing again. He had fallen into the abyss and clawed resolutely back.

During the subsequent year, CBS records negotiated his contractual release from a willing Motown Records. Within the process, he negotiated a workable settlement with the

IRS for his debt. The terms offered a short reprieve and enabled Gaye's return and re-appreciation.

Regaining professional traction, he released possibly the most robust comeback album in history with *Midnight Love* and featured single *Sexual Healing*. The album in January 1983 rejuvenated his career, returning him to elite concert status and opened the window to widely exposed performances and events. Audiences rediscovered Marvin Gaye. His earnings were once again flowing and his legitimacy confirmed by substantial music industry awards.

His career was progressively healing but his soul remained troubled.

Returning to the Los Angeles environment that had once nearly destroyed him, he resumed his cocaine dependence and an exhibition of paranoia-oriented behavior. He sought refuge in his parent's West Adams district home. He had purchased their house from his career earnings. The location is adjacent to the Santa Monica Freeway, concealed by a concrete barrier and strategically planted foliage. The neighborhood is comfortable and unpretentious, but borders the more turbulent South Central Los Angeles battlefields across the freeway.

On Christmas Day 1983, Gaye unwisely presented his father with an unlicensed .38 caliber pistol intended for protection against potential intruders. The volatile relationship between father and son was reignited living within close quarters. Old quarrels resurfaced and painful recollections of a strained coexistence tainted both men. His father's stinging criticisms of his son's secular themed music and previous years of purported physical abuse created a contaminated environment.

His temporary sanctuary became his tomb.

Although Marvin Jr., had experienced the highest strata of professional acclaim, achievement and recognition, within the household, he was merely regarded as his father's defiant son. Family members witnessed his re-ascension into chaos fueled by drugs, erratic behavior and suicidal tendencies.

Family conflicts are rarely straightforward. Each member's personal interpretation even less so.

On the morning April 1, 1984, his parents quarreled over an apparently misplaced insurance policy letter. Marvin Jr. intervened. The son sided with his mother. Threats and shouting escalated. Words were replaced by shoves, kicks and violence. Was the childhood victim turning upon the aggressor?

Shortly after noon, Marvin Gay Sr, terminated the dispute. He entered his son's room with the drawn and loaded .38. He targeted his son's heart and fired twice. Marvin Gaye, Jr. died instantly. He was 44-years-old.

Most of the family members rallied around their father's actions. At trial, one of his brother's confided that the killing was Marvin's suicidal wish. An autopsy concluded that Gaye had traces of cocaine and PCP in his system. Gaye's father claimed self-defense and wept uncontrollably when notified he had slain his son. A month and a half following the shooting, a benign tumor was discovered and removed from the base of his brain. Had the tumor contributed to his erratic response?

A plea bargain agreement to voluntary manslaughter enabled the father a suspended six-year sentence and five years of probation. He did not serve a jail sentence. His wife reportedly filed for divorce the day following the shooting although she posted his bail for release. He died fourteen years later of pneumonia in a Long Beach retirement home, his own ministry long abandoned and forgotten. He publicly expressed remorse for the shooting until the end of his life.

The world lost a talent with perhaps more to contribute by his senseless killing. Sadly even Jesus Christ remarked that a prophet is *never honored in his homeland*. It is possible Marvin Gaye, Jr. had additional profound works left to provoke and inspire listeners into greater levels of enlightenment.

It is equally likely that his own drug usage had emptied his message. The visionary may have been exhausted and had nothing of consequence remaining to compose.

Marvin Gaye Killing:
2101 South Gramercy Place, Los Angeles

PHOTO:
The murder site

A Billionaire Financial Scam That Squandered A Million

In terms of naming articulation, the *Billionaire Boys Club* (BBC) wasn't deficient in ambition. Unfortunately, their investment acumen proved uniquely adept at earning fictional funds, losing actual money and attracting the participation of a shrewder con artist.

Leader Joe Gamsky, later changed to Hunt, assembled an assorted collection of peers from the Harvard School for Boys based in Studio City. Unlike Hunt's Van Nuys middle-class origins, the majority were sons from wealthy families.

Hunt's persuasiveness, charisma and confidence were grounded in the misperception that he had graduated from USC in only two years and successfully traded commodities on the Chicago Mercantile Exchange. In fact, he had dropped out of USC after three semesters and been suspended from trading on the Exchange due to unsound trading practices.

The assembled social and investment club accumulated funding primarily from their member's families. Members dressed extravagantly, rented posh offices, shared luxury apartments, and socialized in upscale clubs. Their investment projects lost nearly $1 million over a single year due to inexperience and poor management. As their funding dried up, Hunt felt he had discovered his savior in freelance photographer Ron Levin, residing in Beverly Hills.

Levin convinced Hunt that he would transfer $5 million into a brokerage firm for the BBC to manage. Hunt reportedly parlayed the investment on paper into $13 million. He was then informed by the brokerage house that there had been no upfront $5 million deposit. The phantom accounts in Hunt's name had been set up by the company to assist Levin's purported project of creating a documentary film about commodities trading.

The ruse proved fatal for Levin. On June 6, 1984 he was reportedly abducted and slain from his Beverly Hills residence by Joe Hunt and *bodyguard* Jim Pittman. He was obliged to draft a $1.5 million check under duress from a Swiss bank account. Levin's body has never been recovered. The check bounced.

In a desperate frenzy to acquire needed liquidity, BBC members devised a plan to squeeze member Reza Eslaminia's estranged father for funding. The 56-year old Hedayat Eslaminia was an Iranian exile and former high-ranking official in Iran during the Shah's regime in the 1970s. He reputedly possessed a $30 million fortune that his son sought to acquire *immediately*. As with every other element of the BBC's operations, the process became flawed from the outset.

In July, Joe Hunt, Dean Karny, Ben Dost and Reza Eslaminia kidnapped the elder Eslaminia living in the affluent San Francisco suburb of Belmont. Their intention was to transfer him to a rented house in Los Angeles, torture him in the basement until he transferred his assets to the group and then murder him. He was packed in a steamer trunk, but the punched in air holes were taped shut to silence his screaming and moans. He suffocated in the back of a pickup truck driven by Hunt on the drive along Interstate 5. His body was buried in Soledad Canyon in remote Angeles National Forest.

After his death, the BBC prepared conservatorship papers for Reza Eslaminia. He and Dosti were dispatched to

Europe for an ultimately futile search for assets. They remained in Europe after the arrests of Hunt and Pittman. Both were apprehended upon their return to the United States in 1985 to stand trial.

In 1987, Joe Hunt and Jim Pittman were put on trial for Ron Levin's murder. A jury found Hunt guilty and sentenced him to life in prison without the possibility of parole. Pittman's trial and a subsequent retrial ended in hung juries. Before this third trial, prosecutors offered him a deal where he would plead *guilty* to be being an accessory to murder after the fact and possession of a concealed weapon. He was sentenced to his jail time already served amounting to 3 1/2 years. In May 1993, Pittman admitted on a television program that he was the individual who shot Levin. Four years later he died of kidney failure at the age of 44.

Dean Karny was granted immunity from prosecution and entry into the Federal Witness Protection Program. He would lead investigators to the remains of Hedayat Eslaminia. His testimony proved crucial in convicting two of the participants during their 64-day trial beginning in November 1987. Their jury required ten days of deliberation before reaching a verdict.

Ben Dosti and Reza Eslaminia were found *guilty* of kidnapping and second-degree murder of Reza's father. Joe Hunt's fate in this case resulted in a hung jury. He represented himself at trial. Dosti and Eslaminia were sentenced to life imprisonment without parole but freed in 2000 when their guilty verdict was overturned. Their convictions were voided based on the grounds that jurors heard a tape never officially entered as evidence.

Facing a new trial, Dosti pleaded *guilty* to manslaughter

and kidnapping and was sentenced to the nearly thirteen years he had already served. Eslaminia did not face re-trial because defense attorneys would not be able to cross-examine Dean Karny. He remained unidentifiable in the witness protection program and reportedly had become a licensed attorney.

Reza Eslaminia continued to proclaim his innocence for involvement with his father's murder. He found it challenging, however to remain free of trouble. In July 2002, he was arrested for driving on a suspended license and possession of cocaine, heroin and a hypodermic syringe during a traffic stop. He avoided potential deportation and three years in state prison. Instead he was given a suspended sentence of one year in jail followed by five years of probation.

In May 2013 a warrant for his arrest was publicized nationally for a vehicular manslaughter charge dating back to August 2012 in the Tenderloin district of San Francisco. The taxicab he was driving ran a red light, hit a car and spun out of control. His vehicle struck and killed a 39-year old pedestrian.

Leader Joe Hunt remains the sole incarcerated participant. He still insists that Ron Levin is alive and likely fled the United States to escape a pending FBI investigation into his financial practices. He has indicated that numerous eyewitnesses have viewed Levin in public, although proof has never been verified. He has repeated attempted to shorten the length of his sentence and emphatically has offered his exceptional prison behavior and founding of a prison spiritual group as proof of his complete rehabilitation. He is presently incarcerated at the Valley State Prison in Chowchilla.

A film, television mini-series and numerous media reportages have shaped the public perception of Joe Hunt and the Billionaire Boys Club. Performer Pharrell Williams and a Japanese company named NIGO in 2005 introduced a men's street wear clothing line called the *Billionaire Boys Club*. Capitalizing on the notoriety of the name, this form of exploitation has continued without protest. In our celebrity-obsessed culture, inappropriate taste appears trivial in comparison to marketing name recognition.

Ronald Levin's Abduction Site
144 South Peck Drive, Beverly Hills

PHOTO: Ronald Levin's apartment complex

Richard Ramirez: The Devil's Ambassador

The *Original Night Stalker* successfully eluded capture for over four decades, while maintaining an absence of public recognition.

Richard Ramirez terrorized Californians via highly publicized home invasions between June 1984 and August 1985. The serial killer, rapist and burglar became the second and more recognized *Night Stalker* in California by a morbidly fascinated media. Ramirez spouted satanically motivated oaths while committing his callous attacks. He employed diverse weapons including handguns, knives, machetes, tire irons and hammers. The attention that his exploits generated diverted investigative and public attention away from the original killer.

Ramirez's confirmed fatalities included Mei Leung, Jennie Vincow, Maria Hernandez, Christina and Mary Caldwell, Dayle Okazaki, Tsai-Lian Yu, Vincent and Maxine Zazzra, Harold Wu, Edward Wildgans, Peter Pan, Elyas Abowath, Bill Doi, Mary Louis Cannon, Joyce Nelson, Lela and Maxon Kneiding and Chainarong Khovananth. He seriously wounded, violated and traumatized numerous other surviving victims.

Ramirez epitomized the extremes of evil, but not intelligence.

His ruthless but careless attacks left innumerable clues, eyewitnesses and finally a license plate sighting of his vehicle. His law enforcement traced mug shot from numerous prior arrests was broadcast nationally via multiple medias. He had casually followed the public scrutiny of his crimes, but did little to conceal his identity. His sole attempt at evasion was once tossing out an identified size 11 1/2 pair of tennis shoes into the ocean.

Ramirez impulsively chose victims randomly. Despite the intensive public manhunt, he simply continued his aimless and drifting lifestyle. His capture was precipitated when he casually strolled into his own arrest.

Ramirez was naively unaware of his public notoriety. He boarded a roundtrip bus in an unsuccessful attempt to visit his brother in Tucson. Upon his return, he casually exited the terminal located in East Los Angeles. Miraculously he eluded police surveillance that was concentrating on outbound buses.

A group of elderly Hispanic women identified him when he slithered into a nearby convenience store. He fled immediately. A chase ensued by neighborhood residents. Ramirez unsuccessfully attempted to carjack multiple vehicles. He was subdued, severely beaten and held by the assemblage until police finally booked him into custody.

Courting the media for maximum exposure, Ramirez achieved a macabre celebrity status. He fed mesmerized reporters with quotable quips, a blood scrawled pentagram on his forehand and exhibited a complete absence of remorse. His trial and sentencing required over a year. He was convicted on 13 counts of murder, 5 attempted murders, 11 sexual assaults and 14 burglaries. A jury convicted him and he was sentenced to death. He died in 2013 of complications from B-cell lymphoma, while awaiting an execution at San Quentin that potentially may have extended his life decades.

Foolish supporters cultivated a morbid fascination via correspondence with this brazen unrepentant criminal. Ramirez married while incarcerated.

Richard Ramirez residence during Los Angeles killing spree: Hotel Cecil, 640 South Main Street, Los Angeles. Killings Committed: San Francisco, Los Angeles Glassell Park district, Rosemead, Monterey Park, Whittier, Monrovia, Arcadia, Sierra Madre, Glendale, Sun Valley and Diamond Bar

The Botched Robbery and Hostage Fiasco at a Rodeo Boulevard Retail Institution

Wednesday June 25, 1986 began as another workday at the lavish Van Cleef & Arpels jewelry store on Rodeo Drive in the heart of the Beverly Hills. At 10 a.m. promptly, an employee unaware of his intentions buzzed Steven Livaditis into the showroom.

Livaditis intended to expediently rob the store and dash to his escape. Four months earlier he had successfully robbed another Las Vegas jewelry store. Beverly Hills proved more problematic. As he was exiting the store, the police department was already responding to a call that a robbery was in process. Livaditis spotted the approaching officers and returned to the interior of the three-story store taking five hostages.

Over the next 13 1/2 grueling hours, a standoff resulted with Livaditis fatally stabbing security guard William Smith in the middle of the back for taunting him with *You think you are a big man with that gun.* Smith bled to death in front of the hostages. He later executed saleswoman Ann Heilperin after police refused his demand to make a televised statement on the news. Under the cover of darkness, he attempted an escape from the building tied together under a blanket with a store employee and a shipping clerk. The botched escape ended in the arrest of Livaditis at 11:30 p.m. He was carrying a briefcase filled with $2 million worth of watches, jewelry and loose gemstones.

Store manager Hugh Skinner, visible as a shield during the escape attempt was shot fatally by a Los Angeles County sheriff's marksman. Skinner was mistakenly fired upon based on erroneous information given to the shooter that the only Caucasian male on the scene was the gunman. Both Livaditis and Skinner were Caucasian, but over forty years difference in age.

Skinner had worked at the Beverly Hills store for over a decade. The store operated under very tight security. Clients walked into a gated area and pressed a buzzer before being admitted. A television monitor scanned each potential customer and then the store manager personally escorted each into the store. Livaditis apparently passed the screening with disastrous consequences.

The 22-year-old Livaditis declared to the *Los Angeles Herald Examiner* in an interview shortly afterwards: *I'd rather they just executed me and get it over. I dread living this type of life. I appreciate freedom.* When asked about what motivated his actions on that fateful June 1986 day thirty years later, he tearfully confessed *I was an evil person.* He is currently incarcerated at San Quentin Prison on death row.

His attitude towards longevity changed. He filed a lawsuit in the US Court of Appeals claiming that he was provided ineffective representation in the penalty phase of his trial resulting in a death penalty sentence. His appeal was formally denied in August 2019.

Van Cleef & Arpels Robbery
300 North Rodeo Drive, Beverly Hills

PHOTO: Van Clef & Arpels Building

The Mickey and Trudy Thompson Morning Driveway Execution

Marion Lee *Mickey* Thompson was an undisputed icon of American off-road racing fame. Maximum acceleration was his forte. Establishing land speed records during his 20s and early 30s, he channeled his obsession into winning numerous track, hot rod and dragster championships. He later formed sanctioning bodies for the sport.

At the height of his renowned on March 16, 1988, he and his wife Trudy were gunned down at their hillside home in Bradbury. A pair of unknown assailants, waiting outside of the Thompson's gated house, committed the precisely timed killings. While preparing to depart for work in the morning, Mickey opened the garage door for his wife to pull out. As he approached his own car, he was wounded and dragged out to his driveway.

Unknown to Trudy, she began to back her vehicle out into the driveway. She was shot dead in her car. The shooter then returned to Thompson and finished him with a bullet to the head. Both assailants pedaled bicycles away to their escape.

The execution involved neither robbery nor any other apparent motive. For thirteen years, the mysterious case remained open without resolution.

In 2001, a former business partner, Michael Goodwin was charged with orchestrating the murder. He was convicted in 2004 on two counts of first-degree murder and sentenced to life imprisonment without parole.

The evidence was entirely circumstantial. Goodwin's reported role was to have hired the killers and assisted them

251

with logistical details in the planning stages. He became the prime suspect based on the nature of previously reported threats against the Thompson's. In reported comments he had made to associates, he expressed an absolute certainty that he would never be caught.

A curious aspect of his arrest was that the charges were filed in Orange County instead of Los Angeles County where the murders were committed. The Orange County prosecutor initiated the proceedings within their jurisdiction citing that Goodwin planned the murders there. The Los Angeles County district attorney's office had refused to file charges against Goodwin claiming there was an absence of incriminating evidence.

Physical evidence tracing Goodwin to the shootings such as payments, telephone records or any eyewitnesses to direct meetings with the shooters was unavailable. Goodwin was identified as being present in the neighborhood with binoculars and another person a few days before the murders. The defense team claimed that the prosecution witnesses including an ex-girlfriend of Goodwin were unreliable.

Motive ultimately became a determining factor. A district attorney's office and jury concluded that Michael Goodwin was the sole individual with sufficient self-interest to order a killing for hire. Goodwin is currently imprisoned at the R.J. Donovan Correctional Facility. The shooter(s) have never been identified.

Despite a life dominated by speed, the expediency of capture and justice for the Thompson's killers has proven excruciatingly protracted.

Mickey and Trudy Thompson Executions:
53 Woodlyn Lane, Bradbury

PHOTO:
Driveway murder site

A Stalker's Fatal Obsession With A Rising Starlet

Robert John Bardo was not an average passive 19-year-old celebrity stalker. He began his odyssey into obsession with infatuations of singers Debbie Gibson, Tiffany, child peace activist Samantha Smith and actress Rebecca Schaeffer.

He admitted to a clinical police and forensic psychologist that he was inspired by another stalker, Arthur Jackson who in 1982 stabbed actress Theresa Saldana repeatedly at her home. Saldana had appeared in the film *Raging Bull*. She survived the attack and eventually continued her acting career. In 2016, she died of complications from pneumonia. Jackson received the then maximum prison sentence of twelve years for his act.

Bardo selected Schaefer as his prey and previously attempted to gain access to her on the set of her television series *My Sister Sam*. He was turned away by studio security. Later he hired a private investigator to locate her residential address. The service identified her residence through California Department of Motor Vehicle records.

The 21-year-old actress was born and raised in Oregon and began her career as a teen model. She moved to New York City to further her prospects in the entertainment industry. She earned a role in the soap opera *One Life to Live*. Her most notable part later came as Patti in the television situation comedy *My Sister Sam*. She returned to California in 1986 and settled in West Hollywood

She appeared in the film *Scenes from the Class Struggle in Beverly Hills* and was cast for a future role in Godfather III. *My Sister Sam* had aired forty-four episodes between 1986-88. Viewing her love scenes in *Class Struggle* propelled Bardo into a jealous rage, vowing to possess her

254

by killing her. He had previously dropped out of high school to undergo mental health treatment and was unable to purchase a gun because of his condition. He convinced his brother to obtain a .357 magnum for him.

On July 18, 1989, Bardo knocked on Schaeffer's front door holding a card her publicist had sent him, her photograph and a copy of the book *The Catcher in the Rye*. She answered the door, politely smiled, listened to his introduction and then dismissed him.

Her response didn't satisfy his expectation. He returned an hour later and when she answered once again, he pointed his pistol at her chest and fired without comment. She screamed *Why, Why?* before collapsing and dying.

Bardo fled Los Angeles and returned to his hometown of Tucson, Arizona. He was apprehended the following day running down the freeway aimlessly shouting *I killed Rebecca Schaeffer*.

At trial, his attorneys employed a mental illness defense, but the prosecution characterized him as *obsessed* rather than *insane*. He was found *guilty* of first-degree murder and sentenced to life in prison without the possibility of parole. In 2007, he was stabbed eleven times by a convict at Mule Creek State Prison. He is currently incarcerated at Avenal State Prison.

In 1990, California passed the first ever anti-stalking law making the act a felony with a mandatory state prison sentence. The law was eventually enacted in all 50 states. In 1994, Congress passed the Driver's Privacy Protection Act that prohibits state Departments of Motor Vehicles from disclosing home addresses of state residents.

Neither of these actions could return Rebecca Schaeffer to the living, but they protected future individuals and celebrities from obsessive and threatening behavior putting their lives in jeopardy.

Rebecca Schaeffer's Apartment
120 North Sweetzer #4, West Hollywood

PHOTO: Rebecca Schaeffer's Apartment Building

Lyle and Erik Menendez: The Sins of the Son's Bury Their Father

For many, it is inconceivable that the avarice and greed of two brothers could callously destroy the lives of two parents who'd lavished on both an unimaginable life of prosperity and wealth.

Yet these very gifts became the motive for murder.

It may be understandable that two siblings, Lyle and Erick Menendez, then aged 21 and 18 years old respectively, might seek an accelerated inheritance. Their impatience might even seem more urgent if they lacked the determination to earn their own wealth. Such ambitions have adequate precedent.

The most striking element behind the savagery of shooting their parents on August 20, 1989 was the ferocity behind their aim. Jose Menendez, their father, was shot point blank in the back of the head with a 12-gauge shotgun. Kitty, their mother, was shot in the leg, causing it to fracture. She was then finished off with shots in the arm, chest and face, leaving her unrecognizable. Both parents were strategically shot in the kneecaps to simulate a professional hit.

Professional hitmen have little need to fire at kneecaps once a victim has been effectively immobilized and dispatched. The multiple firings and placements were more indicative of intense hatred towards their objects.

It becomes difficult to dissect the relationships within an American family, particularly one with prevalent ease and comfort.

Jose Menendez was an accomplished entertainment

industry business executive. He arrived in the United States at the age of 16 following the upheaval of the Cuban Revolution. He attended college in Illinois, met his wife and earned an accounting degree in New York. He elevated his professional success through executive positions at Hertz and RCA. He was being elected as CEO of LIVE Entertainment, most notable for Carolco Pictures, known primarily for violent action films.

The boys enjoyed a privileged upscale childhood. Both exhibited average grades during their academic years. Lyle was suspended from Princeton University based on allegations of plagiarism. There is no accurate gauge precisely how happy or dysfunctional the family operated. During the murder trial, numerous observers offered conflicting opinions. Four individuals know the truth. Two are dead.

The Menendez Brothers planned the killings loosely based on their simplistic arrogance they would never be caught. They arbitrarily tossed the murder weapons. The pair attempted to construct an alibi following the killings. They had intended to view a feature film. It was sold out. They ended up at an alternative film creating time gaps. They met with friends at a local restaurant following the showing and officially returned home around midnight.

They telephoned police to report the murder and play-acted their devastation and grief. Investigators immediately considered them prime suspects but had little evidence to base their suspicions. Neither was tested for shotgun residue on their hands. The home security system had not been tampered with.

The cloud of suspicion hung over the brothers as they spent lavishly, foolishly and traveled internationally. Neither remained in the family's Beverly Hills residence, preferring separate penthouse apartments in Marina del Rey.

Their united front dissolved when younger brother Erik related the murders to his psychologist. His indiscreet confession was accompanied by a death threat. The therapist informed police of both.

Each was arrested and remanded without bail. They were segregated from each other.

Their initial trial was broadcast nationally on *Court TV* during 1993. The television production stimulated more theatrical drama than justice. Erik's defense team defamed both parents in the vilest of degenerate terminology citing a lifetime of sexual abuse, cruelty and pedophilia provoking the killings. The dead cannot respond. The tactic temporality succeeded with the jury deadlocked on conviction.

The brothers were immediately retried and the judge forbade cameras in the courtroom. The jury rejected the abuse defense and concluded that the murders were committed with the intent of gaining immediate control over their parents' considerable wealth.

Both brothers were convicted on two counts of first-degree murder and conspiracy to commit murder. The jury discounted the death penalty due to their lack of a felony background. Both were sentenced to life in prison without the possibility of parole. Each is currently isolated from other prisoners.

The brothers have unsuccessfully appealed their conviction on the state and federal levels. Both have married while incarcerated (Lyle twice).

The three spouses will never enjoy the wealth that marriage might once have enabled. Lyle and Erik are both now interned at the R. J. Donovan Correctional Facility since 2018 after having had no contact before with each other for over a decade.

The poverty accompanying their present and future circumstances is bitter compensation for the wealth of their father they could not secure prematurely.

Menendez Couple Murder:
722 North Elm Drive, Beverly Hills

PHOTO:
Menendez house murder site

Del Shannon: Failing to Recapture The Magic

Del Shannon's success and enduring reputation might be best condensed by a single recording session on January 21, 1961. On that day, he recorded his most popular hits *Runaway* and *Hats Off To Larry*. Using the *Musitron* synthesizer as a lead instrument, *Runaway* soared to the number one hit song on the Billboard record charts that same year. *Hats Off To Larry* would peak at the fifth position later in the year. *Runaway* would become his signature work over a musical career that spanned three decades.

Born Charles Westover in Grand Rapids, Michigan, his stage name was derived as a hybrid from a local wrestler Mark Shannon and his favorite car, the Cadillac Coupe de Ville. Shannon's musical formation was influenced by country western music. Following a stint in the US Army stationed in Germany, he returned to Battle Creek, Michigan finding work as a rhythm guitarist for a local band.

Over the next two years, he assembled his own touring and recording group, enjoyed immediate success and spent the rest of his life futilely attempting to recapture his earliest allocates.

He enjoyed modest success in the United Kingdom, but his subsequent American releases languished on the periphery of commercial popularity. During the 1970s, he was often an opening act for more prosperous performers and ceased touring for periods due to his alcoholism. Over his career, he enjoyed sporadic acclaim as a music arranger and producer. His own haunting lyrics bemoaning heartbreak seemed to mirror the disappointment, restlessness and stagnation of his life.

Upon the death of Roy Orbison in December 1988, there were rumors Shannon might join the group the *Traveling Wilburys* consisting of Orbison, Bob Dylan, George Harrison, Jeff Lynne and Tom Petty. He had collaborated previously with Lynne and Petty. The opportunity never materialized.

Shannon had suffered from depression during the years leading up to 1990. On February 3, 1990, he performed in Fargo, North Dakota at a memorial concert for Buddy Holly, Ritchie Valens and The Big Bopper. Fargo was where their ill-fated February 3, 1959 plane was scheduled to land for a concert that would never take place upon the plane's crash and their deaths. The play list was doubtlessly identical to thirty years of concert performances with no new additions. Five days later, he died from a self-inflicted gunshot wound at his home. Posthumously, the Wilburys recorded a version of *Runaway* and music institutional Halls of Fame would honor him.

Del Shannon's Residence
15519 Saddleback Road, Canyon Country

Christian Brando: The Hellish Consequences Behind A Privileged Upbringing of Neglect

During Marlon Brando's brilliant six decade long career, he was credited with a distinctive depth of acting that often blurred the distinction between performance and his true personality. Midwestern born and raised, Brando was credited with bringing a *natural* approach to acting he credited to the instruction of Stella Adler who taught techniques from the Stanislavski method. This system of action was drawn from internal and external influences of the character being portrayed.

Despite his acting acclaim which began in New York City during his early twenties, his lifestyle was chaotic and relationships messy. The actor was responsible for at least eleven children, five by his three wives (Anna Kashfi, Movita Castenada and Tarita Teriipia, each ex-actresses), three by his Guatemalan housekeeper and three from extra-marital affairs.

The fallout from such disheveled boundary lines, distinctly affected the destinies of his eldest son Christian and one of his daughters Cheyenne. Christian's mother was Anna Kashfi and Cheyenne's Tarita Teriipia who he'd met while filming *Mutiny on the Bounty* in 1960 in Tahiti.

On the evening of May 16, 1990, Christian Brando fatally shot his half-sister Cheyenne's boyfriend Dag Drollet in the living room of one of his father's houses in Beverly Hills. Cheyenne was 8 months pregnant with Drollet's child. Dag was the 26-year old son of a Tahitian bank president and politician. Earlier on the fatal evening, Christian met Drollet for the first time who had flown in a few days earlier to visit Cheyenne.

Over a restaurant dinner, Cheyenne started on a bizarre tangent with Christian relating that Drollet had been physically abuse to her. Returning to the Brando residence intoxicated, Christian confronted Drollet armed. According to Brando, the pair struggled over control of the gun, when it accidentally fired into Dag's face wounding him fatally.

Christian Brando was initially charged with murder, but the key witness for the prosecution to prove premeditation was Cheyenne. She returned back to Tahiti where her father had her admitted into a psychiatric hospital. She refused to return to Los Angeles to testify against her half-brother. Christian agreed to a pleas bargain deal for a reduced charge of voluntary manslaughter and a ten-year prison sentence. He served five years at the California Men's Colony in San Luis Obispo before being released.

Cheyenne would give birth to Drollet's son and name him Tuki. At the time of her boyfriend's death, her life had already begun to spiral out of control. The year before, she had a furious argument with Drollet, borrowed Christian's Jeep and raced erratically down a Tahitian roadway exceeding 100 mph. She barreled into a ditch causing massive facial disfigurement. Her father flew her to Los Angeles to undergo significant reconstructive and cosmetic surgery.

The accident followed by Drollet's death pushed her towards expanded drug abuse, suicide attempts and inconsolable depression. At the age of 25 on Easter Sunday 1995, one year before Christian's release, she hung herself at her mother's house in the village of Faa'a, Tahiti.

Following his prison release, Christian Brando relocated to Washington and reportedly worked as a tree cutter and sculptural welder. His name resurfaced publicly following the 2001 murder of Robert Blake's spouse Bonnie Lee Bakley. She had become pregnant during simultaneous relationships between Brando and Blake and informed each of them they were the responsible party. A DNA test subsequently confirmed Blake as the father. During Blake's murder trial, his legal team attempted to introduce evidence that Brando arranged her murder. The presiding judge prevented the defense from introducing that theory to the jury. Brando refused to testify as a witness citing Fifth Amendment protection and was citied for contempt of court.

On July 1, 2004, Marlon Brando died of respiratory failure from pulmonary fibrosis with congestive heart failure at the UCLA Medical Center. He was also suffering from failing eyesight due to diabetes and liver cancer. At the time of his death, he was working on the preproduction stages of a film project entitled *Brando* and *Brando*.

Christian married twice, the first time to make-up artist Mary McKenna that ended in divorce following six years. He remarried in 2004 for ten weeks to Deborah Presley, an actress who claimed to be an illegitimate daughter of Elvis Presley. The marriage was annulled as Brando pleaded no contest to spousal abuse, placed on probation and ordered to undergo drug and alcohol rehabilitation.

His participation would never be completed. On January 11, 2008, Christian Brando was admitted into the Hollywood Presbyterian Medical Center with an advanced case of pneumonia. He died fifteen days later at the age of 49. The tangled destiny of four tormented lives had completed their full circular orbit.

Dag Drollet's Murder Site
2840 North Beverly Drive, Beverly Hills

PHOTO: Entrance to Dag Drollet Murder Site

Rodney King: Extreme Police Violence Ignites an Excessive Aftermath

The March 3rd, 1991 excessive beating of Rodney King by four members of the Los Angeles Police Department (LAPD) revealed an existing ugly reality of racial profiling and brutality employed by certain department personnel. The officers' controversial violence might have ultimately been dismissed as hearsay had the beating not been captured vividly on a civilian video camera. The ghastly footage of an utterly vulnerable suspect being struck senselessly was distributed and covered globally by news media.

Preceding the violence, King was speeding on the Foothill Freeway (Interstate 210) in the northern San Fernando Valley just past midnight. He and two friends in the car had been watching basketball and drinking. King knew that his elevated alcohol intake would classify him for a DUI (Driving Under the Influence) citation, violating his parole conditions from a previous robbery conviction. He decided foolishly to attempt to outrun the California Highway Patrol (CHP) continuing through residential streets at excessive speeds. His impaired and flawed decision creating catastrophic consequences. The Highway Patrol pursuit was soon joined by several police cars and a police helicopter. Following an eight-mile chase, he was cornered.

The threesome in the car were ordered by one of the CHP officers to exit the vehicle and lie face down on the ground. The two passengers followed instructions and later claimed that they were manhandled, kicked, stomped and threatened. King initially remained in the car. When he emerged, he was reported to have patted the ground, waved at the helicopter overhead and grab his buttocks. The two CHP officers interpreted his bizarre response as reaching for a weapon. As one approached him with his gun to arrest him, the ranking LAPD officer now at the scene informed the CHP officer they would assume control of the situation.

At this juncture, all parties employed the worst-case scenario judgment. Four officers attempted to subdue and restrain King using a swarm tactic. King resisted by standing vertically to remove two draped officers across his back. He was then tasered twice and apparently rose again attempting to either flee or attack one of the officers. He was tasered once again and then struck repeatedly by batons and kicked in his joints, wrists, elbows, knees and ankles. Ultimately 33 blows struck a finally incapacitated King involving eight officers. He was placed in handcuffs and cordcuffs restraining his limbs and then dragged like a carcass on his abdomen to the side of the road. There he awaited the arrival of emergency medical services.

The damning video was filmed after the first series of tasers. The raw footage was offered two days later to the LAPD headquarters at Parker Center. No one appeared interested in viewing the video. Television station KTLA ran the videotape after cutting ten seconds of blurry footage before the image was in focus. What would have been undoubtedly a forgotten abuse was soon viewed globally as an indictment of excessive police violence.

King was transported to Pacifica Hospital after his arrest where he was found to have suffered a fractured facial bone, broken right ankle and multiple bruises and lacerations. In his future negligence claim and lawsuit against the LAPD, King alleged that he had suffered eleven skull fractures and permanent brain damage. One glance at King's swollen face after the beating or worse, viewing the video made his claims hard to dispute.

The City of Los Angeles ultimately did not pursue criminal charges against King for driving while intoxicated and evading arrest. At his civil trial against the city, the jury awarded him $3.8 million along with another $1.7 million for attorney's fees.

The Los Angeles County District Attorney charged the four LAPD officers during the spring of 1992 with assault and use of excessive force. Due to extensive media coverage, the trial was relocated to Simi Valley. Testimony from Pacifica Hospital nurses claimed that the police officers accompanying King joked openly and bragged about the number of blows they had each struck him. The jury unwisely acquitted all four officers of assault and three of the four for using excessive force. They could not agree on a verdict for the fourth policeman.

The reaction over the perceived unjust verdict triggered immediate outrage internationally. Within hours, violence ignited riots in African-American neighborhoods prompting chaos, burnings and looting as the rage spread into adjacent areas. Over six days, the riots would be responsible for 63 deaths, 2,383 injuries, over 7,000 fires and damage to an excess of 3,000 businesses. In the midst of the carnage, Rodney King made a television appearance in which he implored: *I just want to say-you know-can we all get along?*

His simplistic appeal seemed futile amidst the excessive expressions of violence. Even President George H. W. Bush questioned the wisdom of the verdict based on viewing the video.

The Simi Valley trial did not cease the legal liability of the four police officers. A federal trial of the four in 1993 convicted two and acquitted the others. The guilty pair were sentenced to 30 months in prison. All four would be eventually fired by the LAPD and with the exception of one, relocate entirely out of the region.

Los Angeles Police Chief Daryl Gates was pressured into retiring shortly afterwards. He was credited with pioneering several law enforcement innovative programs, but criticized over his perceived racism and insensitivity towards ethnic minorities. He shifted the blame to his command staff for the Los Angeles riots for letting the riot get out of control during its early hours. He remained defiant and seemingly in denial until the end that the violent manifestations were the by-product from years of simmering resentment. He died from cancer at the age of 83 in 2010.

King's two car passengers received minor settlements in lawsuits against the City of Los Angeles. Bryant Allen received $35,000 and the estate of Freddie Helms $20,000. Helms died in a Pasadena car accident in June 1991 at the age of 20. For Rodney King, his $3.8 million settlement failed to resolve his inner demons or keep him away from trouble.

He invested a portion of his settlement into a record label that went bust and was subject to further arrests and convictions for driving violations. He continued to struggle with alcohol and drug addiction. He made periodic television show appearances discussing his problems with adaptation following the beating. One of the stranger follow-ups was his 2010 announcement that he was planning to marry Cynthia Kelly, one of the jurors in his civil lawsuit against the City of Los Angeles. The ceremony would never take place.

On June 17, 2012, Kelly found King lying underwater at

the bottom of his swimming pool. It was the identical fate suffered precisely 28 years before by King's father. He was pronounced dead on arrival at the Arrowhead Regional Medical Center in Colton, California. His autopsy stated that he died of *accidental drowning* with a combination of alcohol, cocaine and marijuana discovered in his system as contributing factors.

Rodney King's ultimate legacy has been difficult to define. His name became a symbol of police brutality, but whether he was simply an innocent victim or contributing factor has been questioned for over twenty-five years. With perhaps the exception of the perpetrators and their supporters, few can imagine how anyone could deserve such abuse once they were incapable of resistance.

Rodney King Beating Site:
Dirt Lot, Osborne Street at Foothill Boulevard, Lake View Terrace

PHOTO: Beating location

The Ultimate Agony Prompted By A Signature Opening Line

Herve Villechaize endured a lifetime of taunting, humiliation and physical pain before finally terminating his life in September 1993 at the age of fifty. Villechaize was born to an English mother and French father who was a surgeon in Toulon.

He was born the youngest of four sons with dwarfism, attributed to an endocrine disorder. His father attempted unsuccessfully to cure the disease via several French institutions. Villechaize was bullied at school due to his short height and found solace through painting. At sixteen, he entered the Ecole des Beaux-Arts to study art. Five years later, he moved to New York City and reportedly acquired his English skills through television viewing.

He continued with his painting and photography and found periodic acting roles. His breakthrough performance came in 1974 when he was cast as the villain *Nick Nack* in the James Bond film *The Man With the Golden Gun*. Global recognition arrived with his role as Tattoo in the television series *Fantasy Island*. His signature line was pointing skyward upon each guest stars arrival and shouting enthusiastically with his heavily French accented *Ze Plane! Ze Plane!*

This unfortunate catchphrase dogged him mercilessly until the conclusion of his life. His time on *Fantasy Island* between 1977-1983 proved unsettling as he developed a reputation for constantly propositioning women and quarreling with the producers. He was eventually fired from the production after demanding an equal salary as his co-star Ricardo Montalban. After he left the series, he acted sparingly and did some voice over work. The extended

272

periods of inactivity resulted in worsening his depressive moods.

During his years of acting prominence, he was active with movements dealing with child abuse and neglect, reportedly going to crime scenes to console and comfort abuse victims. Villechaize understood their trauma as his own intense agony had prompted him towards multiple suicide attempts.

He had married twice and by 1993 was living with his long-term girlfriend Kathy Self in North Hollywood. In the early morning hours of September 4, 1993, his anger and agony climaxed. He left a suicide note to Self indicating that he was unable to continue living with his lifelong health issues. He turned on a tape recorder and began speaking into a microphone a personal message to her. In a sitting position, Villechaize leaned against a sliding glass patio door and placed a pillow against his chest. The tape recorder caught the sound of him cocking the pistol. He fired the gun into his chest shattering the glass door and with the bullet eventually lodging in a kitchen wall.

On tape, Villechaize was heard mumbling *It hurts, it hurts...I'm dying, I'm dying.*

From his final symbolic action, many individuals finally realized that mimicking and mocking Villechaize's signature opening was neither amusing or without cost to his sensitive soul.

Herve Villechaize's Residence
11537 Killion Drive, North Hollywood

PHOTO: Herve Villechaize's Former Residence

River Phoenix: Conventional Excess Replaces An Unconventional Upbringing

During River Phoenix's abbreviated life and rise to fame, he was cast in 24 film and television appearances. He began acting at the age of ten. His charm, talent and vulnerability enabled him to bridge the often-turbulent waters between child acting and younger adult parts. His future as a dramatic and character actor appeared limitless. He was already acknowledged with best acting awards from the Venice Film Festival along with the National Society of Film Critics.

Born on August 23, 1970 as River Jude Bottom, his parents named him after the *river of life* from Hermann Hesse's novel *Siddhartha*. The family lived an unconventional vagabond existence with River never attending formal school.

When he was three, his family joined a religious movement called the *Children of God* and were assigned as missionaries to Caracas, Venezuela. Disillusioned by the cult's sex oriented philosophy, the family relocated to their mother's parent's home in Florida and changed their surname to *Phoenix*. The phoenix is a mythical bird that symbolically rises from its own ashes signifying a fresh beginning.

The family would move again to southern California, where the parents worked at more conventional jobs. River's brother and three sisters often performed with him on street corners for money and food to supplement the family's existence. Ironically, a talent agent spotted the foursome in Westwood and charmed by their talents began representing them. River immediately was hired for commercials and soon was cast in varying dramatic roles in television and film. The critical success and his acting portrayals in the films *Stand By Me, Running on Empty* and *My Own Private Idaho* established his professional credibility and financial stability for his family.

A significant drug addiction and numerous enabling friends accompanied his dash towards stardom. In late October 1993, River returned to Los Angeles from Utah to complete three weeks of interior shooting for his final film *Dark Blood*. He spent his final week binging on a variety of drugs including heroin and cocaine without necessary recovery sleep.

On the evening of October 30th, he performed with a band called *P* at the Viper Room in West Hollywood composed of Flea from the *Red Hot Chili Peppers*, actor Johnny Depp and two other notable musicians. Depp was a part owner in the nightclub.

That evening, cocaine freely circulated amongst the band. Despite an existing heroin high Phoenix freely indulged. He complained to a bandmate during their performance that he didn't feel well and feared that he had overdosed. His complaint was dismissed casually and the band continued playing oblivious to him. Phoenix shortly afterwards got into a scuffle with another patron and was pushed out of the club's side door by a bouncer. He then stumbled and fell onto the pavement and began convulsing.

His younger brother Joaquin dialed 9-1-1 and an ambulance transferred him to Cedars-Sinai Hospital. The band finished their set as the ambulance arrived unaware of what had transpired. River was pronounced dead on Halloween morning at 1:51 a.m. from a heroin and cocaine overdose.

Joaquin Phoenix has become an accomplished actor and producer earning a Grammy and, Oscar, Golden Globe Award and three additional Academy Award nominations. He has struggled through his own bout with alcoholism and a 2006 near fatal jeep crash in the Hollywood Hills.

No one can accurately speculate what acting achievements and accomplishments River Phoenix might have achieved with sobriety. Unrealized talent and wasted potential is always tragic, especially when the blame is self-induced.

River Phoenix's Overdose Site:
Viper Room: 8852 West Sunset Blvd. West Hollywood

Heidi Fleiss: And Yet Another Hollywood Madame

During the late 1980s and early 1990s, Heidi Fleiss evolved into the newest incarnation as a *Hollywood Madame*. She began by managing an existing prostitution ring under another operator named *Madame Alex* (Elizabeth Admas) at the age of 22 before severing her ties three years later.

For two and a half years, her operation flourished and she cultivated a discreet celebrity and wealthy clientele. As her revenue mushroomed, attention towards her operation intensified. In 1993, she was arrested on multiple charges including *attempted pandering*. In 1994, Federal charges were filed against her operation as her state trial concluded. She was found *guilty* in her California trial, but the conviction would be overturned two years later.

One may avoid criminal prosecution through superior legal representation, but the loose ends of her financial empire ultimately proved her undoing. In September 1996, she was convicted of federal tax evasion and sentenced to seven years in prison. She served only 20 months in the Federal Correctional Institution in Dublin, California. She was transferred afterwards to a halfway house and mandated to perform 370 hours of community service. She was released from the halfway house in September 1999.

Her life since incarceration has included several unsuccessful attempts to regain public exposure. Writer F. Scott Fitzgerald wrote in his notes on his novel *The Last Tycoon, There are no second acts in American lives*. The three years of Fleiss' fleeting notoriety lasted even longer than her novelty and actions merited.

Heidi Fleiss' Former Residence
1270 Tower Grove Drive, Beverly Hills

PHOTO: Entrance to the former Fleiss residence

The Nicole Brown-Simpson and Ronald Goldman Murders: An Over-Publicized American Travesty

Blind justice and dispassionate judgment became just another spectator during the 1996 murder trial for the arraigned killer of Nicole Brown-Simpson and Ronald Goldman.

Lost amidst the circus performance and innuendo factory that constituted the publicly televised trial, judgment regarding two homicides was determined. Suspected murderer, ex-husband O.J. Simpson, was acquitted by a criminal jury. The following year, he was found liable for the two deaths in a less publicized civil suit brought by the victims' families. The compensation award of over $33 million dollars will never be fully paid by Simpson.

The amount of the award raised the perpetual question as to what is the appropriate financial measure for a stolen life. Money, revenge and hyperbole characterized the tragedy behind the killings and an attempt to bring a responsible party to accountability.

The twin verdicts proved far from straightforward decisions. Public opinion had predominately convicted Simpson, a once popular former professional football player and television personality. The perception of the publicly charismatic Simpson changed with revelations about his private life. The polished glean of the idyllic, approachable hero became forever tarnished by disclosures of previous spousal abuse, drug use and marital infidelities.

The criminal jury's decision revealed a chronically gaping racial divide within America. Suspect O.J. Simpson was of African-American origin. Nicole Brown-Simpson and Ronald Goldman were Caucasian. Their racial orientations should have been irrelevant in determining guilt or innocence. However, Simpson's defense lawyers accentuated this significance. The tactic influenced the outcome.

O.J. Simpson and Nicole Brown-Simpson had married in 1985 following an eight-year relationship commencing when he was still married. The couple had two children together and contentiously divorced in 1992.

On the evening of June 12, 1994, Brown was killed at her condominium in Brentwood, approximately three blocks away from the neighborhood's most famous former resident, actress Marilyn Monroe. Slain with her was acquaintance Ronald Goldman, present after returning eyeglasses she'd inadvertently left earlier at the restaurant he worked at nearby.

The ferocious stabbings were ghastly. Blood splattered indiscriminately. Footprints, a glove and other incriminating evidence were strewn everywhere. Simpson's alibi proved dubious. Considered immediately a suspect of interest, Simpson impulsively attempted a surreal escape in a white Ford Bronco cruising leisurely south along interstate Highway 405. The captivating moment became pure theatrics as Simpson held a pistol to his temple and threatened to pull the trigger. He didn't.

He eventually instructed his friend who was driving, to return to his residence where he voluntarily surrendered for questioning. The act, interpreted as an admission of guilt, proved not only premature, but a foreshadowing of the absurdity to follow.

Considered arguably the most sensational murder trial of the 20th century, the legal proceedings were broadcast daily over an excruciating eight-month television run. A mesmerized international audience followed every banal element including evidence introduction procedures and live courtroom witness cross-examinations. Excessive expert analysis and commentary over every minute detail of the trial dominated the media headlines. Reputations were inflated, withered and courtroom performances graded. The anticipation for a verdict announcement created more tension than any comparable Academy Award ceremony.

When a verdict of not guilty was announced, a secondary wave of emotion gripped global spectators. Many felt betrayed by a judicial process that had failed two innocent murder victims. Others felt vindicated that an individual of color could be acquitted against insurmountable odds. The polarity of interpretation was usually determined by an individual's own racial orientation.

The prosecution team was generally panned for their failure to secure an apparent straightforward conviction. The trial affirmed that clear-cut convictions are nonexistent against a well-prepared and financed legal defense team of specialists. Their failure to convict Simpson was attributed to their substandard jury selection and inability to clearly demonstrate conclusive guilt. Defense lawyers were able to create suspicion amongst the jurors that the investigative team of the Los Angeles police force planted and mishandled evidence. The fact that there was a substantial amount of evidence not introduced made the jury's decision even more complicated.

At the non-televised civil trail, the jury expediently and unanimously convicted Simpson based on that suppressed evidence which was introduced. Both trials exhibited the best and worst extremes of the American judicial process. Several participants emerged as temporary celebrities. Most ultimately receded back into anonymity. By the conclusion, the overexposure of the case and travesty of the proceedings inflicted a public viewing hangover.

O.J. Simpson would escape criminal punishment but not adverse karma.

His life following the adverse civil suit decision became a series of misdemeanor infractions coupled by his attempted financial evasions from the Internal Revenue Service, representative lawyers and two families awarded damage revenues.

In 2007, he was arrested for leading an armed group of men into a Las Vegas hotel/casino to reclaim signed sports memorabilia by force. A year later, he was convicted of multiple felony counts including criminal conspiracy, kidnapping, assault, robbery and using a deadly weapon. He was sentenced to a 33-year prison term with the possibility of parole following nine years. The sentence appeared excessive based on the severity of the crime. Few observers were astonished by the ironical twist. Most of the arrested participants testified against him. He was incarcerated for nearly nine years at the Lovelock Correction Center in Nevada.

Amidst the whirlwind of the initial O.J. Simpson's arrest and trial, *Time Magazine* flagrantly darkened his facial image on their front cover and titled the issue *An American Tragedy*.

O.J. Simpson will never stand trial again for the murders. The American constitution protects individuals against double jeopardy or being criminally tried multiple times for the identical crime. Announcements regarding a continuing investigation into the double murders have become nonexistent. The entrance gate to Nicole Brown-Simpson's condominium is currently shrouded in vegetation and the address number absent from public view. O. J. Simpson's former residence has been demolished and since rebuilt due to the notoriety.

The Los Angeles Police Departure was convinced that they arrested the correct culprit. The American judicial circus ultimately set him free.

Nicole Brown-Simpson Murder:
875 Bundy Drive, Brentwood

Hugh O'Connor: The Punitive Cost of Drug Addiction

Hugh O'Connor was born in Rome, Italy and became the adopted son of actor Carroll O'Connor when he six days old. O'Connor was filming *Cleopatra* in Rome and Hugh was named after Carroll's brother who'd died in a motorcycle accident the year before.

Hugh was diagnosed with Hodgkin's lymphoma when he was sixteen and survived the cancer with two surgeries and chemotherapy. He began taking prescription drugs for the pain and marijuana for the accompanying nausea. Over time, he became addicted to stronger drugs that despite stays in rehabilitation clinics, he remained unable to cease his dependence.

He followed his father in the acting profession earning roles in two television series *Brass* and his father's production *In The Heat of the Night*. He married a wardrobe assistant from that show in 1992 and fathered a son the following year. On the day of his third wedding anniversary, March 28, 1995, he telephoned his father from his house to tell him that he was going to end his life. He felt that his drug addiction was impossible to overcome and he could not endure another drug rehabilitation program. Carroll immediately called the police who upon arriving discovered that he had just shot himself to death. His toxicology report indicated that he had cocaine in his blood.

Several hours after Hugh's death, Carroll denounced publicly the drug dealer, Harry Perzigian who had been furnishing his son. The week before his son's death O'Connor had provided the Los Angeles Police Department with evidence to implicate Perzigian for drug distribution. He was arrested the day after Hugh's death when police raided his apartment and discovered cocaine and drug paraphernalia.

In the aftermath, Perzigian was sentenced to a year in prison and three years of probation. He sued O'Connor in 1997 for defamation and slander. He lost. He was attacked near his Brentwood residence shortly afterwards by an unknown assailant approaching him from behind a shrub. He died in disgrace and obscurity in 2014.

For the balance of his life, Carroll O'Connor dedicated himself to speaking out on drug addiction awareness. He lobbied successfully in California to have legislation passed that allows family members of an addicted person or anyone injured by a drug dealer's actions to sue for reimbursement for medical treatment and rehabilitation costs. He died on June 21, 2001 from a heart attack due to complications from diabetes at the age of 76. He was celebrated as one of the finest American actors of the twentieth century, but the loss of his son tormented him during his final years.

He confessed during a television interview on CNN's *Larry King Live* program: *I can't forget it. There isn't a day that I don't think of him and want him back and miss him, and I'll feel that way until I'm not here any more.*

Hugh O'Connor's House
219 Aderno Way, Pacific Palisades

PHOTO: Streetview entrance to the house:

A Farcical Sexual Encounter Parlayed Into a Financial Bonanza

Arguably the most famous case of fellatio became a financial windfall for one prostitute and an anecdotal embarrassment for her john. British actor Hugh Grant rose to international stardom playing the lead role in *Four Weddings and a Funeral*. On June 27, 1995, he was in Los Angeles to promote his newest film *Nine Months* and decided by his account *to take a walk on the wild side* cruising Hollywood's Sunset Strip. He blamed what followed on a *moment of insanity*.

On the corner of Sunset Boulevard and Courtney Avenue, he contracted for $60 with 23-year-old Estella Marie Thompson, known as *Divine Brown* to perform oral sex on him in his car. His *insanity* was selecting a stretch of the strip renowned for prostitution and teaming with Los Angeles Police department (LAPD) vice squad members. Grant drove his rental BMW to a nearby neighborhood at Curson and Hawthorn Avenues to complete the transaction.

The pair were caught by vice officers who walked up to the car and observed the act. The occupants were too distracted to notice. Grant and Brown were arrested and charged with *lewd conduct in a public place*. His mug shot was circulated internationally through the news media. Due to previous arrests for prostitution and violations of her probation, Brown faced a potential sentence of six months in jail. Grant faced the condemnation of his viewing public and the wrath of his long-time girlfriend, British actress and model Liz Hurley for her humiliation.

For Divine Brown, her world evolved immediately. Newspapers internationally sought her out and even besieged her residence the following day. The British

289

tabloid *News of the World* paid her a reported $100,000 for her exclusive account. What more could she elaborate on regarding such a common act of transacting commerce?

She claimed that Grant had told her *I always wanted to sleep with a black woman. That's my fantasy.* His fantasy remained elusive however since his car was not equipped with an accommodating mattress. He pleaded no contest, was fined $1,180 and placed on two years' summary probation. He was ordered to complete an AIDS education program.

She was fined $1,150 for parole violations, obliged to perform five days of community service and sentenced to 180 days in jail. She subsequently claimed that after the Grant affair and her financial windfall, she no longer needed to resume her prostitution work. In September 1996, she was arrested for *loitering* at a Las Vegas hotel after making suggestive comments to undercover police officers and subsequently resisting arrest.

Divine Brown parlayed her sudden good fortune into further paid television appearances, newspaper interviews, endorsements and film work in pornography. The east Oakland native claimed that the proceeds enabled her to put her daughters through private schools and purchase a four-bedroom home in Beverly Hills.

Grant resumed his film career as a leading man reputed for his satirical comic roles. He would remain together with Liz Hurley for thirteen years before separating in 2000. He has since fathered five children with two different women. He married the mother of four of his children, Swedish television producer Anna Eberstein in May 2018.

The entire farce might have been entirely avoided if a more

practiced Grant had solicited prostitutes on a regular basis. According to Brown, Grant caught the attention of the vice squad by repeatedly pressing the brake pedal of his BMW with his foot, causing the brake lights to flash.

Hugh Grant and Divine Brown's Sexual Adventure
Near Corner of Curson and Hawthorn Avenues, Hollywood

PHOTOS: Solicitation site and consummation site

Haing Ngor: An Extended and Consequential Journey Curtailed By A Random Killing

There are profound ironies so confounding amidst the chaos of life. Explanation and understanding become impossible. For Haing S. Ngor, to have undertaken an arduous 13,000-mile journey with death as your constant companion and then to die randomly amidst sanctuary seemed too bizarre to be possible.

Ngor was known principally for winning the 1985 Academy Award for Best Supporting Actor in the film *The Killing Fields*. In the movie, he portrayed a Cambodian journalist and refugee fleeing the mass genocide of dictator Pol Pot's Khmer Rouge. He became the first male Asian actor to win an Oscar and only the second non-professional.

Although the role was his debut performance, the plot and circumstances were familiar. Ngor was trained as a surgeon and gynecologist and practiced medicine in the capital, Phnom Penh. In 1975, the Khmer Rouge seized control of the country and a forced mass exodus was initiated by the regime. The genocide march expelled thousands of urban residents into concentration camps for social re-education.

Ngor was obliged to conceal his education, medical skills and even eyeglasses due to the regime's hostility towards intellectuals and professionals. He and his wife My-Huoy were expelled from the capital. While on their journey on foot in one of the camps, she died while giving birth to their child. Ngor was unable to perform her required Caesarean section. Such an act would have exposed his medical skills and certainly provoked a death sentence for father, mother and infant.

The Khmer Rouge government fell in 1979. Ngor was able

to work as a doctor in a Thailand refugee camp. In 1980 he immigrated to the United States with his niece. He was unable to revive his medical practice and did not remarry.

He was cast as a journalist named Dith Pran in *The Killing Fields*. He was reluctant to act, lacking experience but relented based on a promise he had made to his late wife to accurately portray the Cambodia tragedy to an indifferent world. The film and story impacted millions. His award became a crowning achievement for a necessary message.

Following his Academy award, Ngor acted sporadically and lived frugally in a modest periphery neighborhood of Los Angeles' Chinatown.

On February 25, 1996, three members of a local gang shot Ngor dead outside of his apartment in a bungled robbery. A Rolex watch and gold locket containing his wife's picture inside were the only two personal items missing. $2,900 in cash was left in his pant pocket. Due to the ineptitude of the thieves, there was initial speculation the killing might have been revenge motivated by sympathizers of the Khmer Rouge.

In 1998, the three habitual criminals, Tak Sun Tan, Jason Chan and Indra Lim were sentenced to extended sentences with Chan singled out as ineligible for future parole. Tan is currently incarcerated at the Salinas Valley State Prison. Chan is imprisoned at the California State Prison in Lancaster. Lim is no longer listed in the California inmate database. He was formerly interned at the Correctional Training Facility in Soledad. There is no published indication of his being paroled.

Following Ngor's death, a significant number of acquaintances emerged from the shadows to assert financial claims upon his estate. The bulk of his American assets were squandered in legal fees defending each frivolous claim. A more worthwhile Haing S. Ngor Foundation was established in 1997 following his death as a charitable organization oriented to promoting human rights worldwide and Cambodian history and culture.

Ngor in many published interviews following his academy award recognized the timelessness of his performance. His three insignificant killers could not conceive nor diminish the luster of an enduring legacy that graphically portrayed a catastrophe humanity had chosen to ignore. The power of cinematic exposure remains a powerful educational tool for influencing perceptions and reconstructions of history.

Haing Ngor Killing:
Apartment complex, 945 North Beaudry Avenue, Los
Angeles

PHOTO:
Apartment complex where Ngor was slain

Margaux Hemingway: The Prize and Curse of a Famous Surname

Margaux Hemingway seemingly possessed the stature, beauty and charisma every woman aspired towards and every man desired. She was six feet tall, slender and the granddaughter of one of America's most renowned literary figures, Ernest Hemingway.

Her ascent to stardom and international recognition began while she was still attending high school in Portland, Oregon. She was awarded from Faberge the first million-dollar modeling contract. Her rise was meteoric and by the late 1970s, she was a fixture on the international fashion and party circuit. During these social events, she began a dependence on alcohol and drugs.

The Hemingway name opened doors of recognition, but was accompanied by a curse. Her grandfather had settled in Ketchum, Idaho during 1959 and two years later blew his brains out following severe bouts with depression and chronic pain.

Margaux was the middle child of Ernest's eldest son Jack and altered the spelling of her birth name from *Margot* upon learning the evening she was conceived, her parents had drank a Bordeaux Chateaux Margaux wine.

She was born in Portland, Oregon, but lived for stretches in Cuba, San Francisco and Idaho. Despite her beauty, she struggled with a variety of disorders during her teenage years including alcoholism, depression, bulimia, dyslexia and epilepsy. Her younger sister Muriel, an accomplished actress, added *sexual abuse* by their father towards her and their eldest sister, Joan, nicknamed *Muffet* in a 2013 documentary. At sixteen, Joan was institutionalized with mental illness.

Beneath her soaring recognition, the shadow of her grandfather's tormented self-destruction appeared hovering on the periphery. As the glamour and recognition from her modeling career receded, she branched out into acting roles in forgettable productions. Following a skiing accident in 1984, she gained 75 pounds and in 1987 checked into the Betty Ford Center to address her substance abuse issues.

In May 1990, she appeared on the cover of *Playboy* magazine in a desperate attempt to regain recognition. She participated in various promotional and entrepreneurial enterprises. None lifted her status remotely to the recognition she once enjoyed. Her final project was to host an outdoor adventure series on the *Discovery Channel*.

The reality of her professional decline mirrored the fate of many former celebrities who've discovered how replaceable they've become. Her relations with her parents deteriorated, her two marriages failed within three and six years respectively and worst of all, at an age past forty, the opportunities that launched her career were no longer available. Her plummet had forced her to declare personal bankruptcy.

She had become invisible and yet sources close to her indicated that in 1996 she appeared upbeat and had *gotten herself back together*. A longtime friend claimed that she was with her hours before she died in front of a microphone and 500 people singing at a Hollywood restaurant.

On July 1, 1996 nearing 2 p.m., she was found dead in her studio apartment from an overdose of Phenobarbital. Worse, her body was badly decomposed and the exact date of her death never determined. Publicized reports indicated that she was last seen alive five days before her discovery. The Hemingway hex had ultimately prevailed upon its most strikingly attractive member.

Margaux Hemingway's Residence
139 Fraser Street, Santa Monica

PHOTO: Hemingway Residence

The North Hollywood Doomed Heist and Subsequent Warfare

On the morning of February 28, 1997, Larry Phillips, Jr. and Emil Matasareanu were prepared for combat. Phillips had fitted himself with over 40 pounds of protective equipment including a bulletproof vest and various plate guards for shielding his extremities and organs. Matasareanu was similarly armored. The pair was armed with an arsenal sufficient for a military brigade.

Eight months of planning preceded by two successful armed bank robberies in Littleton, Colorado and Winnetka, California had prepared them for another high-risk operation. The North Hollywood Bank of America branch appeared an ideal target to further their idealized goal of incalculable wealth.

The two had initially met at a prominent Venice gym and shared a passion for weightlifting and firearms. Both had been unsuccessful with a conventional lifestyle. Phillips had been a habitual criminal offender, responsible for multiple unsuccessful real estate scams and shoplifting offenses.

They anticipated the entire Bank of America operation would require eight minutes. As with their previous robberies, they would paralyze and take control of the bank operations by firing their automatic rifles airborne before emptying the safe deposit vaults.

Phillips and Matasareanu ingested tablets of the barbiturate Phenobarbital to calm their nerves before entering the branch at 9:17 a.m. Their protocol was well rehearsed. They immediately seized control by opening fire into the ceiling, discouraging resistance. Matasareanu shot open a bulletproof door (resistant only to small-caliber rounds) and gained direct access to the tellers and vaults. The assistant bank manager assisted in filling the robbers' money sacks. From that point, their carefully orchestrated plan evaporated.

Unknown to them, a passing police patrol spotted their entrance into the bank. A request for back-up assistance was radioed in. Police units began to surround the branch in strategic firing positions. A modification in the bank's delivery schedule left the vault with less than half of the currency that Matasareanu had anticipated. He berated the manager and fired 75 rounds into the bank safe to no avail. His shooting destroyed most of the remaining money. The pair would attempt to flee the bank with slightly over $300,000.

The robbers required twelve minutes to complete their heist. They exited the building surrounded and with police demanding their surrender. The pair surveyed their hopeless predicament and opted to exchange fire.

The robbers' higher caliber armaments initially outgunned the police officers. Police were unable to pinpoint headshots with their limited range pistols due to the heavy spray of return gunfire. Within the first seven to eight minutes of the exchange, numerous officers and civilians were wounded. Matasareanu slipped into their white sedan to attempt a getaway. Phillips opted to remain crouched behind other parked vehicles and considered an escape on foot.

Their tactics were pointless. The sedan had the tires shot out. Matasareanu attempted to carjack another vehicle, but it would not operate as the driver fled with the keys. SWAT teams and television news helicopters were arriving simultaneously on the scene.

The gunfire raged and echoed with the intensity of a war zone. The robber's body armor reportedly absorbed ten direct bullets, but did not deter them from continued shooting. At the conclusion of the gun battle, 1,100 rounds were fired by the two and approximately 650 by police.

Phillips and Matasareanu were hemmed in and vulnerable. They separated. Remaining behind their sedan, Phillips, under constant fire, discharged a round into his chin killing himself instantly. Uncertain why he had dropped his gun, police riddled him with shots once he had fallen.

Three blocks away having relocated, Matasareanu was shot 20 times in the legs, apprehended and cuffed by arresting police. They called for an ambulance, but uncertain if there were additional suspects, delayed the arrival for over an hour. Matasareanu expired from excessive blood loss in agony, swearing profusely and attempting to goad the officers into shooting him in the head.

In the aftermath, his family had the audacity to file a lawsuit against the Los Angeles Police Department for violating his civil rights in allowing him to bleed to death. The suit was dismissed without settlement.

Eleven police officers and seven civilians were injured and numerous vehicles and property were destroyed. No one miraculously, except for Phillips and Matasareanu was killed. Police officers have since been armed with heavier firepower and semi-automatic guns. Today, the shooting sites have resumed their former nondescript neighborhood appearance.

North Hollywood Shootout Bank of America

Shooting Death of Larry Phillips, Jr.: Parking Lot on
Archwood Street Adjacent to Bank
Shooting Death of Emil Mastasareanu: Archwood and
Hinds Avenue

PHOTOS:
Phillips location in the shootout, Matasareanu's final
location

The East/West Coast Vendetta and Killing of Christopher Wallace

The murder of Brooklyn's Christopher Wallace, more renowned as rapper *Biggie Smalls* or *The Notorious B.I.G.* on March 9, 1997, punctuated a purported bi-coastal feud between factions of the warring rap music industry.

The signs for imminent disaster were ominous. Wallace represented the East Coast faction and performer Tupac Shakur the West Coast. Shakur was assassinated on September 13, 1996 in a drive-by shooting on the Las Vegas strip. The killing enflamed a rivalry that escalated shooting violence and threats of retaliation. The warring resembled the savage gang behavior the music frequently sensationalized. Despite the adverse stigma, the rap music industry generates substantial international revenue, youth followings and performing icons.

The orchestrated killing prompted more speculation than resolution. The convenient East/West Coast feud theory offered a convenient explanation. Despite eyewitnesses and a composite drawing of the killer, no definitive answers or arrests were ever made.

Two days before his death, Wallace presented an award to singer Toni Braxton at the *Soul Train Music Awards* to a mixed audience reception. A post-event party, hosted by several music industry organizations on March 9, 1997 was held at the Petersen Automotive Museum in the mid-Wilshire district of Los Angeles.

The party was charged, chaotic and closed early by the fire department due to overcrowded conditions. Wallace left at around 12:30 a.m. with his entourage in two large Suburban SUVs. He traveled with three associates in his car. Record producer Sean Combs and three armed bodyguards rode in the other. A third vehicle tailed the two with his record company's director of security.

Christopher Wallace was seated exposed on the passenger side of his vehicle. This convenience undoubtedly ranks as either the choicest piece of good fortune for his assassin or simply a deliberate set-up. A dark Chevy Impala pulled up alongside Wallace's vehicle at the intersection of Wilshire Boulevard and South Fairfax Avenue while awaiting a green light. The driver, dressed in a blue suit and bow tie, rolled down his window, smiled and raised a 9mm blue-steel pistol directly at Wallace.

Four shots were emptied, one fatal. The lethal bullet entered through his right hip and struck several vital organs. The obese Wallace was rushed to the nearest hospital but died an hour later. His bodyguards reportedly fired no retaliation shots during the Impala's escape.

Immediately following the killing, a stream of conspiracy theories and motives were formulated. Numerous subsequent researched articles and books have fingered various suspects. The investigation has been roundly criticized and reopened for examination but remains unresolved. The truth may never surface. Several of the suspicious sources have disappeared, been killed or incarcerated.

Dead musical artists often command and sustain larger paydays for their producers. The rap music world has a bloody precedent of devouring its prominent frontmen. It has fostered an environment of violence fueled by money, drugs and fashion that have provided ample incentives for this cannibalization.

Christopher Wallace during several media interviews acknowledged the inherent risks involved with his status. Why he was seated in a vulnerable passenger seat, cognizant of this threat, is a puzzling question that defies explanation.

Notorious B.I.G. Slaying:
Stoplight Corner Wilshire and South Fairfax (50 Yards North From Peterson Automotive Museum on Fairfax) Across From City National Bank, Los Angeles

PHOTOS:
Parking garage adjacent to the Petersen Automotive Museum, Fateful corner of Wilshire Boulevard and South Fairfax Street

Brian Keith: A Sturdy Boulder Crippled By Fissures

Actor Brian Keith dramatically represented a steady, reliable, good-natured soul with an affable smile. One of his acting peers described his as a *generous actor, a kind man* and *a true friend*. His sturdy screen demeanor camouflaged personal and professional agonies fueled by tragedies to individuals closest to him.

At the age of six, Brian's actor father, Robert married British actress Peg Entwistle, fresh to Hollywood and film acting. The marriage lasted only two years with Entwistle charging Robert Keith with abuse and neglecting to inform her that he was divorced twice and the father of a son from a previous marriage. Three years following their divorce, Entwistle would mount the H letter on the *Hollywoodland* sign on the southern slope of Mount Lee and leap to her death.

Robert Keith's subsequent marriage to his fourth wife may have contributed towards Entwistle's suicide. Her relationship with stepson Brian was never publicly clarified. Brian may have felt guilt in considering himself an impediment to a successful marriage. Speculation over the suicide's influence on his own life becomes inevitable.

Military service during World War II delayed Brian's entry into the acting profession. He was a decorated marine serving as a radio-gunner in the rear cockpit of a two-man dive-bomber.

Following his discharge, he gravitated towards his father's profession enjoying an extended film and television career spanning over forty years. He worked with some of the industries most recognized performers. Between 1966-71, he was cast as Bill Davis, the patriarch of an orphaned clan in the television series *Family Affair*. His co-stars included Sebastian Cabot and child performers Johnnie Whitaker (cast as Jody) and Anissa Jones (cast as Buffy). Following the series conclusion, Jones' life trajectory utterly collapsed.

Her father had been awarded sole custody of her and her brother in 1973 following a contentious divorce. He died shortly afterwards. She loathed living with her mother and instead moved in with a friend. She began skipping school and her mother reported her to police as a runaway. She was arrested, assigned to juvenile hall and remained in state custody before being released to her mother's care.

During this tenure with her mother, Jones began shoplifting, hanging out at the beach, drinking and cultivating a regressive drug habit. She worked briefly at a beachfront donut shop but suffered humiliation when customers recognized her from her previous television role.

On her 18th birthday, she gained control of her saved television earnings from a trust fund. She and her brother rented an apartment together. Less than six months later, she would be discovered dead from a massive drug overdose at a party. The coroner's report found traces of cocaine, PCP, Quaaludes and Seconal in her system during her autopsy toxicology examination. An additional vial of blue liquid was also discovered nearby but never identified. The death was ruled *accidental*, but the significant doses of ingested drugs suggested suicide as a probability. Less than a year later, rotund Sebastian Cabot would die from a stroke at the age of 59. Eight years later, Anissa Jones' brother would perish from his own drug overdose.

Brian Keith continued acting throughout the 1980s and 1990s often in diminished television roles. In 1997, he was diagnosed with lung cancer and emphysema. He had been a lifelong smoker, but had quit a decade previously. During the 1950s, he had been a spokesperson for Camel cigarettes. Chemotherapy treatments ravaged his health and morale. Rumors of personal financial difficulties surfaced. On April 1997, his 27-year-old daughter Daisy abruptly committed suicide in her Hollywood Hills home.

Ten weeks later, the collective weight of calamity propelled Keith to a decisive and fatal conclusion. He wrote a suicide note indicating his desire to join his departed daughter. On June 24, 1997 at his Malibu Beach residence, he resolutely placed a gun to his skull and pulled the trigger concluding his debilitating spiral. He left behind his wife of twenty-seven years Victoria Young. His body was interned alongside his daughter Daisy's at the Westwood Village Cemetery.

Brian Keith's Residence:
23449 Malibu Colony Road, Malibu

Efren Saldivar's Definition of Assisted Medical Homicide

The curious and bizarre example of Efren Saldivar may serve one day as a preliminary case study in the debate over sanctioned medically assisted suicide and mercy killings.

Saldivar was once a respiratory therapist employed by the Glendale Adventist Medical Center. Working the night shift with minimal staff, he injected terminally ill patients with a paralytic drug inducing either respiratory or cardiac arrest.

What separated his actions from traditional homicides is that each of his victims was unconscious and close to death. His selection process made detection nearly impossible.

Following his employment termination in March 1998, he underwent a crisis of conscience and voluntarily confessed to 50 murders. He later retracted his confession. An internal investigation by Adventist Health, the hospital's corporate entity suggested that the actual number potentially exceeded 120 fatalities.

Proving homicides to the soon dead in court proved difficult. Many families had already cremated the victim's bodies. In search of evidence to obtain a conviction, police exhumed twenty buried cadavers that had died during Saldivar's rounds. Six bodies were discovered to have an excessive concentration of Pavulon, Saldivar's preferential drug.

He pleaded guilty to the six counts of murder on the discoveries in his 2002 trial. He received six consecutive life sentences without the possibility of parole and is currently incarcerated at the Substance Abuse Treatment Facility at Corcoran State Prison.

What blurs the ethics behind his actions is that one day they may become standard operating procedures with appropriate consent. The ethical debate continues as some states have legalized assisted homicides and others are contemplating equivalent legislation.

Efren Saldivar may not survive to witness society's evolutionary position change. Within his lifetime, his sentence may one day appear excessive. His actions however in their context created a fresh interpretation to the term *Angel of Mercy*.

Glendale Adventist Medical Center, 1509 Wilson Terrace, Glendale

George Michael: The Grimy Outing Of A Perceived Male Hunk

On April 7, 1998, the carefully crafted public persona of romantic balladeer George Michael was globally outed by an undercover policeman in a public park restroom. Michael was arrested for *engaging in a lewd act* at the men's restroom at the entrance to Will Rogers Memorial Park. The arrest was part of a sting operation conducted by the Los Angeles Police Department oriented towards suspected male sexual activity ongoing in the facilities.

The fine of $810 and 80 hours of community service became incidental in comparison to the damage ultimately inflicted upon his musical career. Michael's appearance had cast him as a virulent male sex symbol to women for nearly two decades, His subsequent admission to feeling conflictive over his sexual identity paled in comparison to the impact his arrest had upon his female following core. Rightly or wrongly, they interpreted his admission as betrayal, particularly due to the seedy environment in which the revelation was revealed.

His career stalled and in many aspects, never recovered.

Michael's talents as a singer, songwriter, record producer and contract negotiator were indisputable. His creative instincts had guided him flawlessly professionally and predominantly on his own terms. The 1998 arrest initiated a downward spiral resulting in legal troubles involving drug related offenses.

In interviews post-arrest, he declared himself gay and launched himself as an active pro-LGBT rights campaigner and HIV/AIDS charity fundraiser. However, he couldn't fully remove or downplay the taint accompanying his abrupt confessional candor.

He toured for three years between 2006-2008 attempting to reignite his base audience, but many had already abandoned him. He earned significant income from these tours and his ongoing recording royalties. Yet something seemed amiss and his appeal had flatlined.

During the early hours of Christmas day, 2016, Michael was found dead in his London home at the age of 53 from a combination of heart and liver ailments. He was rumored to have gained substantial weight and physically become unrecognizable from his former glamour boy appearance.

George Michael Arrest Site For Public Lewdness:
Will Rogers State Park Men's Restroom
1501 Will Rogers State Park Road, Los Angeles

PHOTO: Men's Public Restroom

The Isolated Unexplainable Roadway Slaying of Ennis Cosby

Before he was publicly disgraced as a sexual predator, hypocrite and ultimately felon, William Henry *Bill* Cosby enjoyed global esteem and respect as an entertainment industry icon and social justice pioneer. His legitimate acclaim had afforded him the admiration and legitimacy of credible social commentary. His once immaculate public and professional perception sadly has come into conflict with his private sexual demons.

During the early morning of January 17, 1998 at approximately 1:25 a.m., Bill Cosby assumed another role reluctantly as bereaved father. In the stillness and dimming of insufficient street lighting, his only son 27-year-old Ennis was shot to death at close range while attempting to change a flat tire on his late model Mercedes convertible.

Ten minutes earlier, he had telephoned a female friend who he was intending to visit, to arrive at the intersection of Mulholland Drive and Sepulveda Boulevard. He had requested her help to illuminate the surrounding background. His appeal proved farsighted but tragically too late. In the interim between his call and her arrival, 18-year-old Ukrainian-born Mikhail Markhasev approached him.

The conversation between the two men has never been publicly reported. It may be presumed that the armed Markhasev demanded either money or the expensive vehicle to carjack. Perhaps no words were actually exchanged and the single fatal gunshot was simply a random killing. Cosby was in the midst of loosening lug nuts. His spare tire was tilted against the dark green car body. His emergency flashers were blinking.

316

Markhasev was apprehended within three months after the killing. Following his conviction the following year, he was sentenced to life in prison without the possibility of parole. Five years after the shooting, Markhasev withdrew an appeal over his conviction as an act of admitting his guilt and contrition towards the Cosby family. He remains currently incarcerated at Corcoran State Prison.

Today, a modified well-lit intersection is easily accessible from the 405 Freeway. The paving, sidewalks and linings have been upgraded. The corner is situated below the stunning Getty Museum of Art and crossed daily by thousands of cars. The improvements make such future chance tragedies less likely.

Mourners internationally grieved genuinely for the Cosby family. The intensely private family accepted their sorrow with dignity and minimal public expression. They exhibited their own act of clemency towards the killer by requesting the prosecution to avoid seeking the death penalty during the sentencing phase. It was an admirable and charitable gesture towards a stranger who had robbed them of an adored family member.

Doomed legacies would ultimately define the two Cosby males. Ironically the accumulated wealth of esteem earned by the elder would vanish equally abruptly within two decades.

Ennis Cosby's Shooting Site:
Intersection of Mulholland Drive and Sepulveda Boulevard
just off Highway 405

PHOTO:
Mulholland Drive Freeway Exit

Phil Hartman: The Shocking Murder and Suicide From An Unanticipated Source

Actors, performers and especially comedians often lead divergent double existences between their public persona and private lives.

Phil Hartman had established impressive credentials in each of these genres and international exposure for his eight seasons on the *Saturday Night Live* television series. Born in Ontario, Canada, Hartman moved to the United States at ten and graduated with a degree in graphic arts from Cal State University Northridge. He was credited with designing album covers for prestigious rock bands before evolving into comedy circles.

For all of acclaim he had accumulated professionally, his private life proved less stable. His third marriage to Brynn Omdahl in 1987 was mired in turbulence. They had two children together. Omdahl, a former model and aspiring actress could never contend with the success of her husband. Her personal demons escalated into drug dependence and violent mood extremes.

On the evening of May 27, 1998, Brynn Hartman shared dinner with a film industry friend at a nearby Encino restaurant before returning home. A heated and extended argument ensued with her husband regarding her drug use and his threat to leave the marriage. He ended the dispute by going to bed and sleeping soundly.

At 3 a.m., intoxicated and fresh from a snorting bout of cocaine, she entered his bedroom with a .38 caliber handgun. She fatally shot him twice in the head and once in his side. Erratically she drove to the home of a friend and confessed. He initially did not believe her. The two drove

319

back to her residence in separate cars. Her friend discovered the body and immediately telephoned police at 6:20 a.m. Upon arrival, the police escorted her friend and the two Hartman children from the house.

Brynn Hartman locked herself in the bedroom and committed suicide by shooting herself in the head.

The shock, disbelief and subsequent tributes paid to Phil Hartman revealed a man genuinely liked and respected for his enormous talents. Notably absent was an anticipated sense of the impending tragedy. The telling observation was that Phil Hartman the individual was the man that nobody truly knew.

Phil Hartman Killing:
5065 Encino Avenue, Encino

PHOTO:
Hartman residence

The Terminal Price for Befriending Robert Durst

Susan Berman should have been a famous and wealthy woman. Fate and deficient choices destined otherwise, instead casting her as a murder footnote. Between the years 1966-1974, she was allegedly paid a total of $4.3 million by the Mafia for her father's interests in casinos and other real estate. Her father was *Davie the Jew* Berman, a Las Vegas mob personality whose claim to fame was replacing Bugsy Siegel at the Flamingo Hotel following Siegel's contract killing.

Her life was shrouded in mystery. She claimed both of her parents died under questionable circumstances. Her father expired on an operating table following a heart attack and her mother overdosed as a suicide one year later.

She had a significant base of friends and acquaintances and always seemed just on the periphery of acclaim. She authored multiple books, numerous magazine and newspaper pieces and was constantly soliciting production companies for screenplay adaptations of her varied projects.

She married once in 1984, but her husband died of a heroin overdose two years later. Walking her down the aisle at the Hotel Bel-Air where the marriage was conducted was one of her steadfast friends, Robert Durst.

Berman had met Durst in 1967 while attending UCLA where she earned her Bachelor of Arts degree. Their curious friendship lasted more than thirty years and ultimately may have prompted her brutal murder.

The 1982 disappearance and presumed murder of Durst's first wife Kathleen McCormack Durst has left a bloody trail

321

of suspicious killings of individuals suspected of knowing too many of the intimate details. Among the casualties have included Morris Black (decapitated and found floating in Galveston Bay), Karen Mitchell, an acquaintance who disappeared from Eureka and Susan Berman.

Berman's insider status was well documented. She knew Kathleen Durst during her own residence in New York City. She acted as Robert's media spokesperson and has been credited with facilitating his public alibi. She was depositioned regarding the case in 1982. Durst promptly faxed the document to investigators when he came under suspicion for the murder.

At what price did her cooperation exact?

In 2000, the district attorney of New York's Westchester County reopened Kathleen Durst's disappearance investigation. Susan Berman was contacted regarding her knowledge regarding the case. Berman, now perpetually and desperately short of funds, made the mistake of confiding with Durst the overtures by Westchester County and her indecision about how to respond.

Durst may have correctly presumed their conversation as a veiled threat. In the months before her death, he provided her with two extensive cash gifts totaling $50,000. The sum may have been intended to purchase her silence. Berman wrote to Durst in November reportedly of her hope that her financial requests to him would not ruin their friendship. Durst, living part time in Trinidad, California (near Eureka) may have driven to southern California for a fleeting visit with a murderous agenda to ensure Berman's silence.

On December 24, 2000, Berman was found executed by a 9mm handgun in her Benedict Canyon rental home. A volume of circumstantial evidence pointed towards Durst including motive. He was not arrested until fifteen years later while incarcerated in New Orleans for a weapons violation charge.

He has been held in the Los Angeles County Jail awaiting trial since November 2016. His fluid trial date began during 2020. The gaunt 76-year-old may not survive the proceedings having suffered from cancer and various health ailments.

Potentially *getting away with murder* has gnawed at him inwardly after nearly four decades of pursuit and his attempts to alter his identity. If karma truly exists, Robert Durst is a prime example of the ravages evil may incur.

Susan Berman's Murder Site
1527 Benedict Canyon Road, Beverly Hills

PHOTO: Susan Berman's Former Residence

A Convincing Performance Behind the Killing of Bonnie Lee Bakley

The trail of circumstance and motive led investigators to a single suspect in the 2001 killing of Bonnie Lee Bakley.

The victim had a history of marital exploitations having wedded reportedly eleven times. During her 1999 courtship with actor Robert Blake, she simultaneously dated Christian Brando, son of actor Marlin Brando. Bakley became pregnant and informed each suitor that the baby was his. The infant was named after Brando but a DNA paternity test proved that Blake was the biological father.

Robert Blake married Bakley in late 2000 and the couple commenced their union under conditions he soon found intolerable and manipulative.

On the evening of May 4, 2001, Blake took his wife to one of his favorite Italian restaurants in Studio City. After the meal, the couple returned to his car parked around the corner from the restaurant. Blake excused himself to return to the restaurant where he had allegedly left his handgun. Bakley waited in the vehicle for an unexpected surprise.

In the brief interim between his return (or possibly upon), Bakley was killed by two gunshot blasts to the head while sitting in wait. Her passenger side window was rolled down indicating that she was likely familiar with her killer. The murder weapon was found in a dumpster a few yards away from the shooting.

Nearly one year later, Blake and his longtime bodyguard Earle Caldwell were arrested and charged with conspiracy in connection with the murder. At trial, two former stuntmen and associates of Blake testified against him.

They each claimed that he'd attempted to hire them to kill Bakley.

The trial began in December 2004 following Blake's imprisonment and house arrest. Neither forensic evidence nor direct ties to the murder weapon were able to implicate Blake. Tests to determine whether Blake's hands had contained gunpowder residue had not been performed by the responding investigative police officers. The defense lawyers destroyed the credibility of both witnesses by citing their prior history of drug use and conflictive points in their testimony.

Three months later, a jury found Blake not guilty. All criminal charges were dropped and he was not retried. Three of Bakley's children filed a civil suit against Blake the following year based on the assertion he was responsible for her wrongful death. The civil trial jury found him liable and he was ordered to pay a judgment of $30 million. In 2008, the verdict was upheld, but the assessment cut in half. In 2010, Blake declared bankruptcy due to debts resulting from his legal fees and tax liens imposed by the state of California and Los Angeles County.

Throughout Blake's extended professional acting career, he was considered very capable and inspiriting. The murder of Bonnie Lee Bakley became either a terrible coincidence of circumstance or one of his finest performances.

Bonnie Lee Bakley Murder Site:
Vitellos, 4349 Tujunga Avenue, Studio City

The Physical Self-Destructiveness of a Punk Rock Iconic Group

The Punk Rock era of commercial music followed a regressive cycle of self-destruction. Sharing the rebellious nature of other rock genres, punk proved the least adaptable to evolution based on its complete rejection of social institutions and compromise. The seeds for disintegration were ingrained from the outset. Longevity was presumed irrelevant

The Ramones became an anomaly forming in 1974 until finally disbanding over twenty years later in 1996. The group's name originated from a pseudonym Beatle member Paul McCartney employed while checking discreetly into hotels. Each band member adopted the surname *Ramone* as a unifying gesture. Dee Dee's real name was Douglas Glenn Colvin and founder, lead singer and original drummer Joey Ramone was Jeffrey Hyman.

The Ramone's distinct sound and rapid-fire style of performance appealed to a devoted and fringe audience. Their fan base expanded significantly over their tenure but mass-market acclaim eluded them. Many cite the group as an iconic symbol of the punk rock movement whose message was most popular with the alienated and disenfranchised.

The four original band members are currently deceased. Joey, who was diagnosed with lymphoma in 1995, died from the disease six years later. Johnny died of prostate cancer in September 2004. Tommy died in July 2014 from bile duct cancer.

Irreverent throughout his life, Dee Dee thanked himself at the group's 2002 induction ceremony into the Rock and

Roll Hall of Fame. In 1987, he experimented performing as rapper *Dee Dee King* on a hip-hop music project. The diversion lasted only briefly as music critics universally panned the effort. He participated in other post-Ramone musical projects that were consistently unsuccessful.

On the evening of June 5, 2002, he was found dead by his wife in his Hollywood apartment from a heroin overdose. He had battled drug addiction and mental illness throughout his adult life.

Several subsequent bands have cited the Ramone's musical influence, even if widespread adoration was absent. As observed by KISS bassist Gene Simmons: *It was a failed band. It doesn't mean they weren't great. It means the masses didn't care.*

Dee Dee Ramone's Apartment
6740 Franklin Place, Apartment #204, Hollywood

Phil Spector: The Crumbling Legacy of a Musical Genius

It appears unthinkable that a music industry icon such as Phil Spector would have squandered fame, prestige and freedom for the haphazardly impulsive killing of Lana Clarkson on February 3, 2003.

The story remains a disjointed puzzle with little coherence or logic.

What has been publicly published is that Lana Clarkson accompanied Spector to his Pyrenees Castle residence that evening out of fascination, curiosity or interest in making a recording industry contact. Her body was found by police, slumped over a chair with a single gunshot wound to her mouth and broken teeth scattered over his carpet. Spector had been observed excessively intoxicated earlier in the evening.

At trial, Spector's driver testified having viewed the fateful gun in his employer's hand and heard a rambling confession to the act. Spector maintained that Clarkson had *kissed the gun* in an accidental suicide. The prosecution introduced evidence from four women that Spector had previously pulled guns on them before while intoxicated when they had refuses his sexual advances.

The jury agreed with the prosecution's contention that his actions were a consistent pattern. He was convicted of second-degree murder in 2008 and sentenced from 19 years to life in prison. He is currently jailed at the California Health Care Facility in Stockton.

Spector pioneered a distinctive production technique incorporating deeply layered tracks of music to create a

Wall of Sound. This background would pulsate with energy behind the vocal tracks. The technique has been widely emulated and employed by subsequent generations of musicians and producers. Spector legitimately earned the label of genius and innovator for his musical vision and unique production arrangements. His audio fingerprint remains ingrained on popular music spanning in excess of fifty years.

As a cruel irony, reports since his prison internment have indicated that he has lost his voice permanently due to laryngeal papillomas of the throat.

His Alhambra based residence was completed in 1927 for the Dupuy family as a retreat funded by their investments in real estate and oil. The property, designed by local architect John Walker Smart rises clandestinely above the squat Alhambra stucco residences. The 8,600 square foot castle features a red tile roof, Italian marble foyer, 10 bedrooms, 8 1/2 baths, secret passages, wine cellar and a host of innovations. In 1998, Spector acquired the mansion following decades of decay, abandonment and vandalism. The sprawling estate enabled Spector the seclusion he desired and an isolated outlet for his addictions and eccentricities.

The notorious mansion has remained unoccupied since Spector's imprisonment and in March 2019 was put on the market with an asking price of five times what Spector purchased it for. The sale was part of a divorce settlement with his third wife, Rachelle Short, whom me married in 2006 while he was in jail and awaiting trial.

Pyrenees Castle Murder:
1700 South Grandview Drive, Alhambra

PHOTO:
Entrance to Pyrenees Castle

The Christmas Eve Massacre by a Santa Impersonator

The lone vacant lot at the end of a Covina cul-de-sac remains peculiar within the vibrant suburban neighborhood. Another real estate valuation bubble has inflated pricing and once again prompted renovation, refurbishment and renewal with the intent for resale.

An empty lot defies entrepreneurial opportunity. Fencing has surrounded the vacant parcel for nearly seven years exhibiting only an expansive lawn, uniformed backdrop trees and a drained swimming pool with accompanying slide. These traces are the sole evidence of former life on the property.

On Christmas Eve 2008, nearing midnight, Bruce Jeffrey Pardo adorning a disarming Santa Claus outfit, knocked on the front door of his former in-laws residence. Pardo was toting a gift-wrapped package and four concealed pistols. A party of 25 people was enjoying the holiday festivities including Pardo's recently divorced wife and family.

Pardo's eight-year-old niece rushed excitedly to answer the door. Uncle Bruce met her attempted embrace with a point-blank gunshot to her face. She miraculously survived. The faux Santa then discharged one of his 9mm semi-automatic handguns randomly into the terrified assemblage. The horror escalated.

Pardo unwrapped his present. The package contained a homemade flamethrower, with which he sprayed racing fuel gasoline around the house in order to set it ablaze. Simultaneously he began executing selected individuals with his handgun. The shootings and inferno ultimately killed nine people and wounded three.

He concentrated his rage exclusively towards his ex-wife's family. The dead included his ex-wife, Sylvia Ortega-Pardo, her mother Alicia Sotomayor Ortega and father, Joseph Ortega. Other fatalities included Sylvia's two brothers, Charles and James Ortega and their wives Cheri Lynn Ortega and Teresa Ortega. Sylvia's sister, Alicia Ortega Ortiz and son Michael Andre Ortiz were also killed,

The intensity of the fire seared most of the victims beyond recognition and entirely destroyed the house. Flames elevated 40-50 feet into the Christmas skyline. Identification of the victims could only be completed via dental and medical records.

The genocide singed the source as well. Pardo suffered third-degree burns before his exit with the Santa suit adhering to his skin and defying removal.

His original planned escape strategy was to Canada. He had taped a significant sum of cash to his body and purchased an airline ticket. The physical agony sustained from the burns likely proved unbearable and altered his plans.

Instead of reinventing a fresh existence, Pardo drove thirty miles to his brother's empty house in Sylmar. He emptied a bullet into his head as a final act of defiance. Before pulling the trigger, Pardo had rigged his rental car for detonation and parked it a block away from his brother's house. It was a symbolically demonic ending for a man with no prior criminal past. Yet he was a man convinced that he had lost everything.

His motives were later traced to a contentious divorce settlement confirmed one week prior to the attack. The massacre was intended to address a litany of grievances and bitterness that had doomed his marriage of only one year.

He had been recently fired for fraudulent billing practices as an electrical engineer.

Simmering beneath a conventional surface, Pardo was a troubled individual ready to detonate. He had stored a significant cache of weapons and incendiary devices in his Montrose home. Their ultimate intended use might have later proliferated into a more expansive expression. The shadows darkening his existence found an initial outlet.

The emptiness of the vacant lot summarizes the vacancy branding his life. Bruce Pardo obliterated an entire family and their residence, but in the process his own identity as well.

Bruce Pardo Killing Rampage Remains:
1129 East Knollcrest Drive, Covina

Michael Jackson: The Perilous and Lonely Descent From Grace

Singer Michael Jackson had ascended the performance mountaintop following a career of four decades starting with his brothers in the *Jackson Five* until launching his own solo career. His songwriting, vocals and dance choreographies elevated him into a status shared by few entertainers in the history of music. Yet despite his success and acclaim, novelty, innovation and fresh faces sustain the industry.

Jackson had attempted to restructure his facial features for a more youthful appearance with disastrous results. His musical playlist remained popular, but he hadn't released any new material for five years and only to marginal response compared to his former standards. His legacy was in danger of fading into nostalgia, as had the careers of two peers, Prince and Elvis Presley. Fearing this descent into irrelevance, he planned an ambitious tour of comeback concerts. The exposure was designed to rejuvenate his worldwide appeal and reverse numerous financial difficulties. On the evening of June 24, 2009, Jackson rehearsed his repertoire and dance choreography at the Staples Center in downtown Los Angeles for his upcoming July London opening.

No one present at the rehearsal imagined that evening would be his last.

On the following morning at 9:28 a.m., actress Farah Fawcett died following an extended battle with cancer. It is unknown if Jackson became aware of her death. His personal physician Conrad Murray administered the anesthetic propofol and anti-anxiety drugs presumably to assist him with sleeping. The dosage proved fatal and his

335

doctor discovered him in his room with a week pulse and not breathing. He administered CPR to no avail while his security service called for an ambulance at 12:21 p.m. He was transferred to the UCLA Medical Center but pronounced dead upon arrival.

The global shock and response behind the news of both deaths stimulated unprecedented activity on the Internet and news broadcasts. At the age of fifty, it seemed inconceivable that the youthfully obsessed Jackson could be dead. A memorial service was held in his honor on July 7th at the Staples Center broadcast globally. An estimated two and a half billion people followed the live broadcast. His formerly stagnant music sales immediately soared and a fresh legion of admirers came to appreciate and rediscover his phenomenal talents. The resurgent interest in his work erased his former debt and stimulated rivers of fresh revenue sources.

Michael Jackson would not profit from his career resurgence or sudden financial liberty. He was gone. His sustained drug use and various eccentricities created a portrait of an artist surrounded by dependants and admirers, but ultimately condemned to a lonely and unsettling hell.

In the aftermath of his death, questions regarding the sequence of events preceding his dying emerged. Two months following his demise, the Los Angeles County Coroner officially declared his death as a *homicide*. In 2011, Dr. Conrad Murray was prosecuted and convicted of *involuntary manslaughter* for his role in administering the lethal intoxication. He served a two-year prison sentence and forfeited his professional reputation and means of livelihood. In June 2018, he resurfaced in media reports regarding the death of Joe Jackson, Michael's father. He characterized the elder Jackson as one of the worst fathers of all time and hoped *that he finds redemption in Hell.*

The irony behind Murray's role in the tragedy was that Michael Jackson would have expediently found a replacement for Murray had he not accommodated Jackson's medication whims. One of the realities of entertainment stardom is there is always someone available and agreeable to assist in your impulsive requests and ultimate decline.

Michael Jackson's Residence
100 North Carolwood Drive, Los Angeles

Ronni Chasen: When Two Divergent Worlds Collide

The divergent universes of motion picture publicist Ronni Chasen and unemployed felon Harold Martin Smith rudely collided shortly after midnight on November 16, 2010.

Smith's vehicle (or potentially bicycle), sidled up to Chasen's late model Mercedes-Benz from the passenger side at the popularly traveled corner of Sunset Boulevard and Whittier Drive in Beverly Hills. It is presumed that Smith intended to rob Chasen who was returning from a film premier. What transpired during the exchange may only be speculated. Chasen probably attempted to drive off and was shot point blank with five hollow-pointed bullets, an unusual form of ammunition employed by someone nearly destitute.

After being shot, her car veered towards a curb and toppled over a concrete streetlight. Investigators found Chasen slumped over in her seat with the steering wheel airbag inflated. She had blood flowing from her nose and chest area. The front passenger side window was shattered from the shooting.

Speculation initially concentrated around various motives for her homicide including a contract killing. None made sense, as she hadn't cultivated any discernable enemies. Smith was a habitual criminal with a background in burglary and drug possession. He had been discharged on parole the previous year. He had confided to neighbors that he was the responsible party for the killing and claimed had done so for money. Police ultimately discounted his claims as simple boasting.

Harold Smith was fingered as a possible suspect based on a tip generated from an *America's Most Wanted* television emission. When investigators approached Smith at his East Hollywood apartment, he turned a gun on himself and committed suicide. The gun was identified as Chasen's murder weapon.

In the end, investigators concluded the killing was the consequence of a randomly botched robbery.

Even amidst the lush atmosphere of wealth and opulence, the divide between rich and impoverished, respectable and criminal is illusionary. For all of the security insulation a life of achievement and compensation brought Ronni Chasen, unforeseen fate intruded into her carefully constructed life.

Ronni Chasen Murder Site
Corner North Whittier Drive and Sunset Blvd, Beverly Hills

PHOTOS: Intersection of the shooting, Light pole that Chasen's car crashed into

Scott Dekraai: The Mad Rampage and Excruciating Slow Justice and Sentencing

A contentious and extended child custody battle involving a couple's 8-year-old son provoked a deadly shooting rampage in a Seal Beach hair salon on October 12, 2011.

The Meritage hair salon became an execution chamber for berserk shooter Scott Evans Dekraai armed with three handguns. The attack, which lasted approximately two minutes, killed six within the salon (two died the day following from their wounds). The victims included Randy Lee Fannin, the shop owner, Michelle Fournier, the killer's ex-wife, Lucia Kondas, Victoria Buzzo, Christy Wilson, Michelle Fast and Laura Webb. Webb's mother, who was having her hair done by her daughter was critically injured by the shootings but survived. Two of the fatalities were customers.

To cap his descent into madness, Dekraai shot David Caouette to death through the front windshield and passenger window of his parked vehicle outside the salon. He had apparently visited a restaurant adjacent to the salon and had no connection to the other victims.

Dekraai's outburst was motivated by an adverse custody decision against him the day before and an argumentative conversation with Michelle Fournier earlier that morning. He methodically shot each victim in the head and chest and would have killed more had several patrons not been able to exit the building or remained hidden in the back room.

Upon storming the salon, owner Fannin attempted to calm the determined Dekraai by pleading, *Please don't do this. There's another way. Let's go outside and talk.*

Words could not placate an individual intent on blood. Carnage was Dekraai's response. He was arrested less than a half mile from the scene in a pick-up truck clothed in body amour. He did not attempt to resist a superior armed police force.

The shock and disbelief within the community resulted in a candlelight vigil the following day and donations to a substantial victim's aid fund. Seal Beach had only one solitary murder during the four previous years preceding the rampage.

The public outrage did not result in swift justice. Later in the month, Dekraai was indicted on eight counts of murder with special circumstances and one of attempted murder. The prosecutor expressed his intention publicly to seek the death penalty. Nearly three years later Dekraai was convicted based on a guilty plea.

The sentencing phase, which would have normally followed, was delayed due to a ruling by an Orange County Superior Court judge in March 2015. The judge cited evidence that Dekraai's constitutional rights had been violated while imprisoned at the Orange County Central Men's Jail. A jailhouse informant had been placed in an adjacent cell to his.

Dekraai was either incredibly indiscreet with his remarks or the informant was exaggerating his access to informed comments. The informant claimed in testimony that the killer had bragged about the homicides in conversations between the two. Whether the placement of the informant was intentional or coincidental, the testimony should have seemed irrelevant considering the magnitude of the act. The judge's ruling indicated his conclusion that the placement of the informant was deliberate.

In the interim, the California Attorney General's office was designated to assume the duties from the county prosecutors. Over two years later, on September 21, 2017, Dekraai was sentenced to eight terms of life in prison without the possibility of parole. The original prosecution teams' mismanagement of jailhouse informant information precluded extending the death penalty to Dekraai.

He is currently interned at the Substance Abuse Treatment Facility and State Prison in Corcoran.

Meritage Salon:
Meritage Hair Salon, 500 Pacific Coast Highway, Seal Beach

PHOTO:
Meritage Salon shooting site

Don Cornelius: Pioneering Ethnic Exposure and Exiting on His Terms

Between 1970 and 1993, Don Cornelius was am imposing host on his television program *Soul Train*. The groundbreaking dance and musical showcase brought wider exposure of African American culture, musicians and dancers to mainstream television audiences. Cornelius appeared as the umber to Dick Clark's more polished *American Bandstand*. His deep husky voice commanded attention and generated street credibility.

He was born and raised on Chicago's South Side and joined the US Marine Corps, serving 18 months in Korea. Post-military service, he sold tires, automobiles and insurance. He briefly became a Chicago police officer before quitting to take a three-month broadcasting course in 1966. The same year he was hired by radio station WVON as an announcer, news reporter and disc jockey.

Cornelius transitioned into television the following year and recognized the existing void in African American programming. Following a news commentary program he'd initiated, *Soul Train* began as a daily Chicago-exclusive show. The novel program entered national syndication and he relocated to Los Angeles.

Cornelius maintained his role as writer and producer throughout the show's duration, which concluded in 2006. He retired from hosting in 1993 due to health concerns. He pioneered numerous catch phrases and his personal appearance altered with the prevalent times and fashions.

He had two sons with his first wife. In 2001, he married

Russian model Victoria Chapman and their martial difficulties escalated into public headlines. In October 2008, he was arrested for spousal abuse and discouraging a witness from filing a police report. His estranged wife obtained two restraining orders against him. In March 2009, he pleaded no contest to the abuse charges and was placed on 36 months of probation. The couple divorced the same year.

For fifteen years preceding his death, Cornelius suffered from seizures, a complication following a 21-hour operation he underwent in 1982 to correct problems with his cerebral arteries. He endured ongoing excruciating pain that factored into his final fateful decision.

In the early morning hours of February 1, 2012, police officers responded to reports of a shooting. They discovered Cornelius lying on the floor in his residence, the victim of a self-inflicted gunshot wound to his head. He was 75 years old. The epitome of cool had ultimately exceeded his capacity for pain tolerance.

Don Cornelius' Residence
12685 Mulholland Drive, Sherman Oaks

PHOTO: Entry gate to Don Cornelius' Residence

Whitney Houston: A Spiraling Fall From The Mountaintop

In May 2000, singer Whitney Houston released *Whitney: The Greatest Hits* to global distribution. The double disc set would sell over 10 million copies and mount her career to its ultimate summit. From a mountaintop, the perspective is downward.

The peak proved perilous for a star that had cultivated an impeccable reputation during her climb. The cracks were already evident during 1999 when her behavior veered erratically. She starting arriving hours late for interviews, photo shoots and rehearsals. She canceled concerts, talk-show appearances and her weight loss became evident. Observers blamed drugs and many pointed explicitly to the cause being her turbulent marriage to singer Bobby Brown.

Despite being financially stable due to a $100 million contract signed with Arista Records in 1998, her personal demons and struggles overshadowed her talents.

Her 2002 album *Just Whitney* received mixed reviews and her final work following a six-year hiatus, *I Look To You* received acclaim but only modest sales. In 2007, she divorced Bobby Brown, but her physical decline continued. Her drug addiction had introduced heart disease into her accumulation of afflictions.

During the second week of February 2012, her *disheveled* and *erratic* appearance foreshadowed her end. She visited rehearsals for producer Clive Davis' post-Grammy Awards party scheduled at the Beverly Hilton Hotel.

On the afternoon of February 11th, Whitney Houston was

347

found unconscious in the bathtub of her suite at the Beverly Hilton Hotel. Paramedics arrived but found her unresponsive to CPR. Her cause of death was officially ruled as *accidental drowning*. Her toxicology report indicated that she had ingested cocaine and other drugs earlier.

Public reaction was shock, but those who had closely witnessed her decline couldn't have been surprised. Curiously, the pre-Grammy Awards party continued as scheduled and Bobby Brown performed his show in Mississippi within hours following his ex-wife's death. Her legacy was feted at an invitation-only memorial service in her hometown of Newark, New Jersey.

Whitney Houston's mezzo-soprano voice and arrangements enshrined her professional star perpetually. Her lone daughter and heir would not enjoy for long her mother's inheritance. Bobbi Krissy Brown indicated her inclination to follow in Whitney's career path as a singer and actress. She would controversially marry Nick Gordon, a close family friend who had lived in their household since he was twelve the same year as her mother's death. She inherited her mother's entire estate, but was not scheduled to receive the bulk until she reached the age of 30.

The inheritance would never be fully transferred. She had been the subject of tabloid and gossip speculation throughout her teen and adult years. Stories about her own drug use and significant weight loss resembled her mother's tortured history.

Similar to Whitney, she was discovered on January 31, 2015 in a bathtub in her Alpharetta, Georgia home. She was found face down in the water. Gordon reportedly performed CPR until emergency medical service personnel arrived.

She remained alive and breathing while being transferred to a local hospital. Her oxygen loss to the brain necessitated the doctors placing her in an induced coma.

Eventually she was transferred to Emory University Hospital, but remained in a coma and surviving on a medical ventilator. She would remain comatose for six months, despite family denials and reports of her improvement. She died in hospice care on July 26, 2015 at the age of twenty-two. The sad saga of mother and daughter concluded when they were buried together at Fairview Cemetery in Westfield, New Jersey.

In 2016, Nick Gordon was found liable in a wrongful death case involving Bobbi Krissy Brown. As part of the settlement, a judge ordered him to pay $36 million to father Bobby Brown's estate. Three years later Gordon would die on New Years Eve in Florida from a drug overdose at the age of 30. His death closed the circle on a tragic string of calamity that merely reinforced the insufficiency of wealth to guarantee happiness.

Whitney Houston Death Site:
Beverly Hills Hilton, Room #434
9876 Wilshire Blvd., Beverly Hills

PHOTO: Beverly Hills Hilton

Tony Scott: A Brother Deviating From the Glittering Path

Brothers Anthony and Ridley Scott shared remarkable trajectories as film directors, producers and screenwriters. Both graduated from the Royal College of Art in London and in 1995 each received the BAFTA Award for Outstanding British Contribution to Cinema. Queen Elizabeth II knighted Tony's elder brother Ridley in 2003. On August 19, 2012 at 12:30 p.m., Tony without forewarning parked his car on the Vincent Thomas Bridge in San Pedro, climbed a fence on the span and leaped to his death into the waters landing near a tour boat.

The Los Angeles County Coroner's Office announced his cause of death as *multiple blunt force injuries* with traces of mirtazapine and eszopiclone in his system at the time. He left behind two suicide notes in his vehicle, but the text of neither was publicly revealed. His autopsy indicated that he had neither cancer nor serious medical conditions that his brother disputed two years later. In an interview with *Variety Magazine*, Ridley indicated that Tony had been *fighting a lengthy battle with cancer*.

The Vincent Thomas Bridge was opened in 1963 as a 1,500 foot-long suspension span crossing Los Angeles Harbor. It rises 365 feet above the water and numerous suicides have been recorded. In October 1990, 1964 Olympic US diving bronze medalist Larry Andreasen was killed jumping from the west tower attempting to set a diving record.

Tony Scott was considered one of the most influential film directors of his era responsible for popular movies including *Top Gun, Crimson Tide, Beverly Hills Cop II, Enemy of the State* and *The Taking of Pelham 123*. Two days before his suicide, actor Tom Cruse accompanied him on location scouting for the sequel to *Top Gun* scheduled for production the following year. He was involved with several upcoming and ongoing television film and projects that made his death seem inexplicable.

In the end, he simply jumped off the carousel on his own terms for reasons that may never be fully explainable.

Vincent Thomas Bridge
Los Angeles Harbor, San Pedro

PHOTOS: Vincent Thomas Bridge

A Son of Anarchy's Lethal Fuselage

Johnny Lewis' signature role for two seasons as biker *Kip Half-Sack Epps* in the television series *Sons of Anarchy* expanded his global acting exposure. The time period also coincided with bouts of regressive mental illness.

On October 30, 2011, Lewis was involved in a high-speed motorcycle accident resulting in severe head trauma. Declining both MRI scans and subsequent psychiatric treatment, Lewis embarked on an odyssey of bizarre behavior culminating in tragedy less than one year later.

He would be arrested three times during 2012. The first was when he struck two men in the head with a bottle during a fight. The second occurred when he broke into a woman's home and the third when his probation officer recommended incarceration for his mental health issues and chemical dependency. In early August 2012, he was granted provisional outpatient status and agreed to a deal with the District Attorney where he would be released for his time already served. He was kept incarcerated an additional two months. The unexpected delay reportedly contributed to a plunge in his morale and one final erratic and unforeseen action.

Five days following his release, police responded to the *Writers' Villa*, a Los Feliz based bed and breakfast property known for hosting up-and-coming performers, directors and writers. Lewis has previously lived there in 2009 and was allowed back. Proprietor, 81-year old Catherine Davis and her cat were found dead inside and Lewis' deceased body sprawled on the driveway.

Neighbors had phoned police after Lewis violently and abruptly attacked two of them coupled by Davis' screams.

Piecing together a scenario of events, investigators determined that he had induced *blunt force head trauma* and strangulation to David before mounting the roof and accidentally or purposely falling.

A follow-up investigation revealed no motive for the killing or intent towards suicide. His death was ruled *accidental*. His toxicology report indicated no evidence of drugs or alcohol in his system. Davis had resisted, fighting back based on fingernail marks on his neck. Observers closest to him speculated that his untreated head trauma might have resulted in a psychological disorder prompting sudden flair-ups of anger and violence. In 2014, *Sons of Anarchy* concluded production following a seven-season run.

Johnny Lewis' Killing Site
3605 Lowry Road, Los Angeles

PHOTO: Former Writer's Villa

Paul Walker's Crash Death: The Blurred Distinction Between Cinema and Reality

The *Fast and Furious* film series is an action film franchise glamourizing street racing with incidental morality infused by the clichéd good and evil characters. The fact that the vehicle chase scenes defy reality or glorify the endangerment of other motorists and pedestrians seem incidental. The films have become wildly popular internationally.

Actor Paul Walker, one of the principal stars of the first seven movies enjoyed a sterling reputation as a performer and personality. In the midst of final shooting for *Fast and Furious 7*, he accompanying his friend and financial advisor Roger Rodas as a passenger in a new Porsche Carrera GT. On Saturday, November 30, 2013, an unremarkable sunny day, they chose a section of Valencia roadway to test the capabilities of the vehicle.

Streaking easterly along an empty straightaway of Kelly Johnson Parkway, Rodas, a professional driver, reportedly exceeded over 100 mph. For reasons never specified, he lost control of the car. The vehicle partially spun around before striking a sidewalk. The driver's side struck a tree followed by a light post. The vehicle continued to spin 180 degrees until the passenger side rammed a tree. The car burst into flames, making any escape impossible and killing both occupants. The carnage appeared to have split the vehicle in half.

The coroner's report indicated that neither drugs nor alcohol were detected in either men and there was no evidence of foul play.

Walker was eulogized throughout the entertainment

industry for his premature passing at forty. His career had expanded substantially from his *Fast and Furious* exposure. His sole heir, his daughter, received a reported $10.1 million from the estate of Roger Rodas. She and Walker's father settled separate lawsuits with the German manufacturer Porsche for undisclosed amounts. The widow of Rodas sued Porsche after the crash but lost in court.

Mislaid apparently in the litigation flurry was the reality confirmed by the investigator for the Los Angeles coroner that *the car was driving at unsafe speed*. There is little point in arguing the idiocy behind aggressive and speeding motorists. They are seemingly unconscious to the damage and risk they pose to drivers daily on West Coast roadways. The saddest observation noted by the deaths of Rodas and Walker was their inability to distinguish between controlled film chase scenes and reality.

Paul Walker's character Brian was retired at the conclusion of *Fast and Furious 7*. More improbable follow-up plots have already followed and will continue to follow. The certainty that excessive speed kills seems oblivious and lost within the context of each filmed morality tale.

Roger Rodas and Paul Walker Crash Site
Hercules Street Near Kelly Johnson Parkway, Valencia

Keith Emerson: The Tormenting Price Behind Perfectionism

Keith Emerson was considered one of the finest and technically accomplished keyboardists in rock and roll history. During his peak as one of the founding members of Emerson, Lake and Palmer (ELP), he was responsible for integrating classical compositions into a rock music format. This synthesis of sound labeled ELP as a *progressive rock* band and earned the ire of more fundamentally hard-core heavy metal, new wave and punk bands.

Emerson's early formation was grounded in a variety of influences including jazz, boogie-woogie and classical music. At the age of fifteen, he acquired his first Hammond organ. His mastery of the instrument made him a popular addition with several bands. He formed *The Nice* group in 1967 and integrated several innovations into his flamboyant showmanship including a Moog synthesizer, explosion-like sounds and various feedback articulations. He was known for beating his organ with a whip, riding across the stage on the organ as his horse, playing while it was atop him and wedging knives into the instrument extending notes.

In 1970, Emerson formed ELP with Greg Lake and Carl Palmer and gained an immediate following after their performance at the 1970 Isle of Wright Festival. Their distinctive sound and multi-leveled compositions made their performances both distinctive and incomparable to other touring acts. Ever the innovator in an industry touting rebellion, Emerson introduced classical compositions to rock audiences that would never have imagined appreciating such works.

One of his most notable live show stunts involved playing a piano suspended 15 to 20 feet in mid-air that rotated end-over-end while he remained seated. Greg Lake confessed the piano was fake and had no inner works, but Emerson deadpanned a response during a 2014 interview noting *I think having a pilot's license helped a little bit.*

Theatrics and special effects aside, the trio were outstanding creative musicians and perfectionists in their collaborations. ELP disbanded in 1979 and each member worked on various musical projects during the succeeding years. They briefly reunited but disbanded later when they were unable to recapture their previous commercial success. Emerson composed several film tracks that proved an ideal fit for his orchestral and classical style.

In 1993, Emerson endured nearly career ending nerve-graft surgery to his right hand. By 2002, he reportedly had regained full use of his hand and could perform with his usual gusto. His public confidence masked extreme inner turmoil. He would have a later operation to remove a bad muscle, but the pain and nerve issues were worsening for him. He was tormented with worry regarding his ability to play music to his elevated standards.

Emerson could not reconcile mediocrity or the equivalent of arthritis in his hand. He made peace with one of his harshest critics, John Lydon (Johnny Rotten) from the punk band *Sex Pistols* who was a Santa Monica neighbor.

On March 11, 2016 at the age of 71, Emerson died from a self-inflicted gunshot wound to the head at his Santa Monica residence. He had been suffering from heart disease and depression associated with alcohol. His inner circle confirmed that his anxiety towards his performance level had ultimately pushed him to his fatal decision. Nine months later ELP bandmate Greg Lake died following an extended battle with cancer.

Keith Emerson's Residence
420 Marine Street, Unit 4, Santa Monica

PHOTO: Keith Emerson's Apartment

Verne Troyer: An Intense Suffering Concealed Within A Caricature

Verne Troyer developed into one of the world's shortest men due to result of cartiliage-hair hypoplasia. The 2 foot 8 inch Troyer was initially raised Amish by two working class parents in southern Michigan. His parents left the faith when he was still a child. Troyer credited his adaptation skills to their treating him identically as his two average-sized siblings.

Growing up on a farmland rural environment, Troyer was fulfilled essential laborious chores and animal husbandry. His introduction to a film career began in 1994 with stunt work for an infant character. He continued stunt performances along with acting minor roles throughout the decade. In 1999, he landed his signature comedic role as *Mini-Me* in the successful Austin Powers film series. He collaborated with Austin Powers star Mike Myers in two additional films. Entering the new Millennium, he acted sporadically and appeared making guest appearances as himself in various reality television series.

The entertainment industry can seem inhumanely cruel to one-dimensional performers. Troyer found his career relegated into limiting caricature and oddity roles. He struggled with depression and substance and alcohol abuse. His lowest ebb became the criticism and fallout from a poorly advised private sex video between Troyer and his former live-in girlfriend.

On April 21, 2018, 49-year-old Troyer's personal demons overwhelmed his diminishing career prospects. He was found dead at his home from acute alcohol poisoning that was later ruled a suicide. Behind his public beaming grin, fans would ultimately realize that the price for being a human novelty was indeed steep and severe.

Verne Troyer Residence:
8005 Teesdalke Avenue, North Hollywood

PHOTO: Verne Troyer's Residence

Author, photographer and visual artist Marques Vickers was born in 1957 in Vallejo, California. He graduated from Azusa Pacific University in Los Angeles and became the Public Relations and Executive Director for the Burbank, California Chamber of Commerce between 1979-84.

Professionally, he has operated travel, apparel, wine, rare book and publishing businesses. His paintings and sculptures have been exhibited in art galleries, private collections and museums in the United States and Europe. He has previously lived in the Burgundy and Languedoc regions of France and currently lives in the South Puget Sound region of Western Washington.

He has written and published over one hundred books spanning a diverse variety of subjects including true crime, international travel, social satire, wine production, architecture, history, fiction, auctions, fine art, poetry and photojournalism.

He has two daughters, Charline and Caroline who reside in Europe.

A scene where someone is killed, their ghost emerges to shake hands and say talk to those around the body

Made in the USA
Monee, IL
30 August 2020